Here I am God, Send my Sister.

11 Women Who Shaped Missions

Here I Am God, Send My Sister.

The Traveling Team Press (PO Box 567, Conway, AR 72033) functions only as book publisher. As such, the ultimate design, content, editorial accuracy, and views expressed or implied in this work are those of the author.

ISBN: 978-0-578-40005-1

In recognition of the time and hard work given by the staff of The Traveling Team, we would like to thank the following people:

Project Manager
Callie Coglizer

Theme and Content Editors
Jessie Smith
Caroline Studdard
Todd Ahrend

Authors
Jessica Ahrend
Ivy Amanda
Caroline Studdard
Sara Bauer
Taylor Marie
Amber Joy
Natalie Crump
Natalie Francis
Abbie Brock
Timera Kakish
Rebecca Hickman

Kylee,

I have been so blessed by your friendship over the past few years. I have learned so much from your faith and boldness to Christ. The way you whole-heartedly follow after the Holy Spirit inspires us all. I pray that this year God draws you near to Him like never before. That you fall in love with Him even more everyday. And that your faith, boldness, and confidence grows ever more. Praying that God speaks to you and guides you clearly and reveals His character to you. And that every day you would die to yourself so that Christ may live fully in you. I picked this book up from one of the speakers at Perspectives. And I as I was reading, I thought of you. Thought you might enjoy hearing their stories. I pray that these stories inspire and encourage you. That they would strengthen you to keep seeker after God. I hope you enjoy it. Praying for you! Congrats on graduating!

For Cheyanne

Hebrews 13:7

3

TABLE OF CONTENTS

Here I Am God, Send My Sister.

YOU ARE YOUR STORIES

We don't get to choose our family stories. Remember that embarrassing picture or that first day of school? Yeah, I'm trying *not* to. Family stories become the museum we walk through to explain who we are–for better or for worse. Every family has them. Maybe you wish you could erase a few of those stories, or all of them! Some stories are stories of joy, others of heartbreak or shame. Stories of delight in how our parents met or what they felt on the day you were born. Or stories of heartbreak like a sudden news of cancer, divorce, or death. Your life has been shaped by a library of comedies and tragedies.

These stories are more than history. They are markers on the path which show us where we come from, but these stories also set a trajectory that point to our future. None of us were born into a perfect story. Deep down we know the path ahead needs some better alignment if we are going to pursue the life God wants for us. But what if you *could* rewrite your family story? What if you *could* exchange the script you have been given for another one? **God doesn't just redeem your soul; He redeems your story.**

GOD DOESN'T JUST REDEEM YOUR SOUL; HE REDEEMS YOUR STORY.

If you are a Christ-follower, you don't just get salvation; you get a new set of stories. God's family stories have power to shape our new identity in Christ. They give you new markers from the past that point to a new path ahead full of faith. Everyone lives out of a family story, but in Christ you get a unique choice. You can choose *which* family stories will shape your future. This is a wonderful gift God has given us in the stories of the Bible, the gift of a new library of family stories driven by faith.

You may be familiar with some of these family stories. People like Abraham, Esther, David, Mary, and the Apostle Paul. There are many more heroes of the faith whose names are not in the Bible, but they are in the family. **Their stories help guide us** toward things like godly contentment, perseverance through suffering, and an unceasing prayer life. When we are struggling to put faith into practice in our own lives, God will use their stories to disciple us in our own walk with Him. And some of the greatest stories of faith and obedience come from those who were pioneer missionaries.

These pages are filled with stories of *real* missionary women who battled enormous odds to get the gospel to some of the world's hardest places. These are your grandmothers and great grandmothers, your aunts and great aunts in the faith. Not all of them faced the same things, but collectively, they faced

7

everything you face today. Things like support raising, parental objections, and singleness are the same obstacles and excuses which emerge as we begin to step out in faith. This book will help! Let their stories challenge and inspire you. Let their vision of how God used them rescript how you envision God using you to change the world.

This "family story" idea is not new. God has been writing it for years. Hebrews 13:7 says, "Remember your leaders, those who spoke the word of God to you. Consider the outcome of their way of life and imitate their faith." God reminds us to look back at these stories and allow them to be a significant tool for growing our faith. He knew we would need heroes to inspire us to stay the course in our own obedience, especially when it comes to something as difficult as pioneer missions.

So welcome to your new family tree. Get to know these women. Share their stories, both the highlights and the hardships. Let their DNA reengineer yours. Their obedience was as much for you as it was for those they reached in their lifetimes.

"IF THESE ARE THE FOUNDING FATHERS OF MY LIFE, CAN I NOW WAVER?"

A young missionary once asked himself, *"If these are the founding fathers of my life, can I now waver?"* With their blood running in the veins of our faith, people who've been waiting to hear the good news of Jesus finally will.

Here I Am God, Send My Sister.

ANN JUDSON

A Cost Counted
By Jessica Ahrend

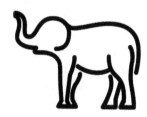

If we're honest, most of us live on a wild pendulum, swinging between two extremes. On the one hand, we desire so strongly to make a name for ourselves. On the other, we shrink into crushing insecurities. And so we swing- thinking too highly of ourselves, swoosh, thinking too lowly of ourselves, swoosh....

Ann Judson held the secret. She didn't think of herself at all. Yet here we are, reading her story. And if Ann were reading with us, she would object, "This is not my story; this is His story."

My native land, my home, my friends, and all my forsaken enjoyments rushed into my mind; my tears flowed profusely, and I could not be comforted. Soon, however, the consideration of having left all these for the dear cause of Christ, and the hope of being, one day, instrumental of leading some poor degraded

10

females to embrace him as their Saviour, soothed my griefs, dried up my tears, and restored peace and tranquility to my mind.

When we begin to have the conversation about women who have made their mark on history, Ann Hasseltine Judson ought to be one of the first names mentioned. Not only was Ann a pioneer of an independent spirit uncharacteristic among women of her day, she also served her husband, her team, the people of Burma, and her Lord with radiant humility. Ann made American history, but truly she is a heroine of Kingdom history.

Our story begins in Bradford, Massachusetts, on December 22, 1789. Rebecca Hasseltine, wife of John Hasseltine, gave birth to the youngest of their five children, Ann. Her personality was happy, curious, eager to learn, restless, and socially insatiable. Often known for being the most entertaining at parties, Ann was always invited. Carefree and light-hearted, she indulged herself with amusements and vanity. Her adolescent years were spent on a "career of folly," thinking only of social activities and what she would wear. She called herself "one of the happiest creatures on earth."[1]

As for her spiritual life, she was raised with a moral foundation that, though disconnected from a true understanding of faith, included attending church and saying prayers. Mostly, her religious education consisted of her mother's instruction on how to be a good girl and abstain from vices. She thought as long as she did the right things she would go to heaven. Only occasionally was her conscience pricked that true spiritual life went deeper than her behavior.

Where she truly shone was in her intellect. James Knowles in his *Memoir of Ann H. Judson* accounts of Ann's life, "Mrs. Judson's mind was of a superior order. It was distinguished by strength, activity and clearness. No one can review her life and read what she has written and published, without feeling her mind possessed unusual vigour and cultivation."[2] Ann was educated at the Bradford Academy in Massachusetts.

During her years at the Academy Ann was exposed to Hannah More's *Strictures on Female Education*. She read this quotation: "She that liveth in pleasure, is dead while she liveth." [3] She resolved to be more serious and focused on Christ. What this really meant was she would not to go to any more parties. She was quite self-assured at this resolution that she certainly had secured for herself right standing with God. Despite all her best fleshly attempts to be pious, she

wrestled, feeling drawn and helplessly attached to the world. Ann simply could not be the person she wanted to be. The glaring hypocrisy between her heart and her behavior nearly crushed her. Then, at age sixteen, the Holy Spirit quickened her heart and did a permanent work of drawing her irreversibly to God. What she could not be on her own was accomplished in Christ! From that time on she'd set a steady course of continual growth and devotion to Christ and His cause.

America at this time had never sent any missionaries. The Declaration of Independence had only been written thirteen years before Ann's birth! In fact, most of America was still undeveloped and was considered a wild frontier. Native Americans inhabited the New World, and Christianizing the natives was always an impulse of English exploration and colonization.[4] David Brainerd was among the first Protestant missionaries to the Native Americans in the 1740s. Though he died at age 29, his life of service had a profound impact on twenty-year-old Ann. She wrote in her journal in 1809,

> Have had some enjoyment reading the life of David Brainerd. It has had a tendency to humble me and excite desires to live as near to God as that holy man did. Have spent this evening in prayer for quickening grace. Felt my heart enlarged to pray for spiritual blessings for myself, my friends, the church at large, the heathen world, and the African slaves. Felt a willingness to give myself away to Christ, to be disposed of as He pleases. Here I find safety and comfort, Jesus is my only refuge. I will trust His word, and rest my soul in His hands. I will depend on Him, not only for the salvation of my soul, but for daily grace and strength to persevere in a religious course. O may I now begin to live to God.[5]

ANN JUDSON HELD THE SECRET. SHE DIDN'T THINK OF HERSELF AT ALL.

This journal entry is among several others in the same year that reveal an undeniable move of God's Spirit in Ann's life. Though she had no predecessor to follow and no formal instruction on the subject, God Himself was directing Ann's heart to be used by Him in the mission field. He was beginning to impress upon her a sense of duty to the lost and yearning to be at His disposal. Only one year later did Ann meet the man who was to be her husband, Adoniram Judson.

Adoniram was already blazing a trail overseas. Though no agency was established, no financial or organizational means existed by which to send him, Adoniram's course was set. He and three other men were petitioning for an American board of missions to be founded so they might be the first missionaries sent to the foreign field by a denomination. The fruit of this petition was the eventual formation of the American Board of

13

Commissioners for Foreign Missions.

Ann was engaged three months after her initial meeting with Adoniram, and on February 5, 1812, the two were married. She writes,

> Though I am unworthy of being allowed to do anything for Christ, I am happy that He has made it my duty to live among them, and labour for the promotion of the kingdom of heaven. O if it may please the dear Redeemer to make me instrumental of leading some of the females of Burma to a saving acquaintance with Him, my great object will be accomplished, my highest desires gratified: I shall rejoice to have relinquished my comforts, my country, and my home.

What Ann endured during their engagement was discouraging. Society had deemed her decision imprudent and wild. All her counsel was opposed to sailing overseas. Yet, undaunted, she pioneered an arduous, grueling, and solitary path for every woman to come after her. She writes during their engagement,

> When I get near to God, and discern the excellence of the character of the Lord Jesus, and especially His power and willingness to save, I feel desirous, that the whole world should become acquainted with this Saviour. I am not only willing to spend my days among the heathen, in attempting to enlighten and save them, but I find much pleasure in the prospect. Yes, I am quite willing to give up temporal comforts, and live a life of hardship and trial, if it be the will of God.[6]

Thirteen days after their wedding, the Judsons and one other couple, Samuel and Harriet Newell, boarded a ship for four months. The trip was a difficult one for Ann who felt as though her heart were breaking from having all of her loved ones and attachments ripped from her. Though she endured this devastating emotional hardship along with the physical difficulties of being sea-sick, Ann remained positive and ever confident of God's call.

The Judson's first stop was in India. They landed in Calcutta on June 17, 1812, and were greeted by William Carey, England's first Protestant missionary.[7] Though they desired to be allowed to stay, people were increasingly opposed to missionaries—especially Americans. Their presence had become strictly forbidden. The Newells sailed first to an island off the coast of Africa, the Isle of France, modern-day Mauritius. Two months later the Judsons arrived. In that time, Harriet had given birth to a daughter, and both she and her daughter had died.

When Ann and Adoniram landed in Mauritius, what they anticipated to be a joyous reunion with their beloved friends and teammates was met with the severe blow of Harriet's death. Ann had lost her one companion in the world in which she now lived. The mission had offered up America's first martyr.[8] Ann was devastated.

> She is gone, and I am left behind, still to endure the trials of a missionary life... Mr. J and I are now entirely alone—not one remaining friend in this part of the world. The scenes through which we pass are calculated to remind us, that this world is not our home, and that we are fast verging toward the grave... Yet we are willing and desirous to live a few years, that we may serve God among the heathen, and do something towards spreading a knowledge of the Saviour, in this benighted world.[9]

Each struggle, each hardship, each trial drew Ann more into Christ as her refuge, her strength—He became all she needed.

Months passed and God's providence directed them through a series of shut doors, to the country of Burma (present-day Myanmar). Though Ann had previously been fearful they might be led to this harsh country, she writes,

> I most sincerely hope that we shall be able to remain at Rangoon, among the Burmans, a people who have never heard the sound of the gospel, or read, in their own language, of the love of Christ. Though our trials may be great, and our privations many and severe, yet the presence of Jesus can make us happy.

They landed on July 13, 1813. Ann writes, "I feel happier than ever, that we have chosen Rangoon for our field of labour, and cannot but hope that we shall yet see the goodness of the Lord, in the land of the living."[10] The population of Burma when the Judsons arrived was seven million and was almost entirely Buddhist. Led by a king, this country was cruel and inhospitable. Felix Carey, son of William and Dorothy Carey, was living in Burma when they arrived and was crucial to their introduction to the basic ways of life.

However deplorable the physical and spiritual environment proved to be, God had made Ann to be a social magnet. After a year she had befriended foreign rulers who had authority in that colony. She quickly became fluent in the language. In September of 1814, Ann gave birth to a baby boy, Roger—the first white child to be born in Rangoon. For the first time, the Judsons were beginning to have meaningful conversations with the Burmese about the gospel. It seemed their long-awaited ministry was beginning to thrive! Then tragedy struck. Eight months after Roger was born, he took ill. With no medical resources available, the Judsons had to watch their precious Roger die. They mourned the loss of their only earthly source of joy.

16

In these early years of the Judsons' ministry, they buried their son, battled bouts of extreme illness, experienced a degree of loneliness to which few can relate, and saw no fruit for their labors. Still they plodded along in language acquisition, translation, and building relationships. Ann was meeting weekly with a group of women to teach them. Adoniram had written a gospel tract, and they had welcomed their first ministry teammates. Furthermore, the missionary zeal their departure had sparked in America was spreading. Missions agencies were being started, and people were being sent.

Ann's contribution to the missionary enthusiasm cannot be underestimated. She was the leading female missionary author of the nineteenth century. She used this influence to shine a light upon the spiritual plight of the East and the urgent need for women's work. Her letters and journals were inspirational to a generation of Americans who had very limited access to the lost world.[11]

After seven long years of ministry in Burma, the Judsons were able to construct a zayat, or meeting place. Ann would join her husband for the teaching of the people. This was a bold but clear approach for the foreigners in this harsh land full of hard hearts. It bore fruit, and soon after they had their first convert! It was Ann's duty to instruct him. More converts began to come until at last they had a little band of believers—the beginning of God's redemptive work in Burma![12]

With a core group of twenty Christ-followers, the Judsons wanted to head inland to a city called Ava. Soon after arrival, war broke out between Burma and the British government in India. This terrible turn of events cast a shadow of suspicion on the American missionaries, and Adoniram was soon captured and taken as a prisoner of war. Whatever trials the Judsons had faced to this point paled in comparison to the absolute extreme of human suffering that lay ahead for the following two years.[13] Each day, Adoniram endured a horrid, dark, vent-less, shackled, vermin-infested existence. He never knew when torture or execution might await him. Each night he was hung by his feet until morning, defenseless against the hungry rats.

All the while, Ann kept a steady presence in the prison. The guards knew her well as she regularly brought food to help keep her husband alive. Even when Adoniram was moved to a different location seven miles away, Ann followed. Her spent, emaciated body endured another pregnancy. After Maria was born, she brought her along to see her father. Ann's relentless effort saved Adoniram's life. She played a major role in the preservation of the first Burmese translation of Scripture—her husband's life's work. This translation is still in use today.

At long last, the war ended, and Adoniram, along with the other prisoners of war, were released. He, Ann, and baby Maria sailed peacefully and free down the Irrawaddy River, back to their mission home. Their reunion was not enjoyed for long. Adoniram's translation abilities were solicited to aid and negotiate the new peace treaty. What they anticipated to be a short separation stretched out over months. In his absence, Ann received a violent fever. At thirty-seven years old, having spent only fourteen years on the field, Ann died. It was said,

> God saw fit to remove her; for her work was done. She had not lived in vain. Her name will be remembered in the churches of Burma. Let us hope, meanwhile, that her bright example will inspire many others with the generous resolution to toil and to die, like her, for the salvation of the heathen.[14]

It is humbling to consider this servant of God who, with single focus, gave the world not a passing glance but sacrificed all for the true treasure of seeing the lost come into the kingdom of heaven. It is humbling to consider that someday, those of us who know Him, will worship God alongside her, and alongside those Burmese brothers and sisters for whom she answered His call. It is humbling to consider the fact that our God–the God of Abraham, David, Paul, and Ann Judson–continues to choose weak and frail humans to do His work on earth.

SHE HAD NOT LIVED IN VAIN. HER NAME WILL BE REMEMBERED IN THE CHURCHES OF BURMA.

Ann Hasseltine Judson is a heroine of Christian history, not on her own merit but because she gave herself fully to the Author of history, to be poured out at His disposal. May we, with the reverent abandon, consider the comforts of this life to pale in comparison to the everlasting joy of having been the vessel of salvation to the lost world!

BETSY STOCKTON

Overcoming Odds
By Ivy Amanda

Does missions ever feel like an impossibility? Does it feel like far too many things stand in the way of you actually ever getting to the field? You're in good company with this woman who rose to the occasion of knocking down every barrier to obedience. Betsey Stockton overcame overwhelming odds to become the first single female missionary sent from America.

Betsey Stockton was a trailblazer. She was the first single female missionary to be sent by a North American mission agency. Regardless of the fact that she never received a formal education, Betsey pursued a career in teaching. She left America to serve as a missionary just a few years after being freed from slavery. Throughout her life, she had to overcome significantly more obstacles than most other men and women in her pursuit of becoming a foreign missionary. Others tried to classify her solely based on her childhood as a slave, her gender, her marital status, or her race, but Betsey chose to focus on the status of her soul and her obedience to the Lord. Betsey Stockton's story is one of honesty, vulnerability, and a deep love for the Lord that eclipsed every barrier she had to overcome in order to serve Him.

Born on a farm in Princeton, New Jersey in 1798, Betsey was the child of a slave in the household of Robert Stockton. Without a record of Betsey's father, there is little known about her family history. In her will, she described herself as a "mulatto," meaning she had some mixture of white and black ancestry. It is believed either her father or grandfather may have been a white man. Most likely Betsey never knew who her father was.[15] As a young girl, she was given as a gift to Robert Stockton's oldest daughter, Elizabeth, who was married to Ashbel Green, a Presbyterian minister in Philadelphia. Following after his father, Dr. Ashbel Green was a strong antislavery advocate of his day. In light of his opposition to slavery, Ashbel and Elizabeth never intended to keep Betsey as a slave.[16] Betsey was not legally freed until later in life, but during her time in the Green household, she was treated kindly and looked back on the Green family with the deepest affection.

In her youth, Betsey was described as "wild and thoughtless, if not vicious," as well as "precocious," and "alarmingly wild and willful."[17] Simultaneously, Betsey was also highly intelligent. Members of the Green household recognized her potential and provided opportunities for Betsey to develop her intellectual abilities. She was taught by Dr. Green and by their youngest son James, but she never received formal education. Betsey was given access to the family library, which she took full advantage of, eventually excelling in many subjects. She was taught arithmetic, English grammar, literature, and composition, and also had a thorough understanding of Scripture, Jewish antiquities, Bible history, and geography. As a young girl, her brilliant mind was undeniable as she was given access to more and more educational resources. She continued to excel. The Green family's decision to invest time into educating this young slave girl would transform Betsey's future. She would go on to educate and empower others for the rest of her life.

Betsey's spiritual life began to transform when the family moved to Princeton in 1812. Dr. Ashbel Green had become the president of what is now known as Princeton University in 1814. A spiritual revival started on campus. Ashbel Green was considered highly influential in the start of the revival. All over campus students were meeting, praying, worshiping, and studying the Bible. In 1816,

Betsey Stockton devoted her life to Christ. She was baptized, and later that year, at twenty years of age, she was legally freed.[18] Betsey continued to live with the Green family and work for them as a hired servant.

The spiritual revival on campus had a much broader scope than the immediate community around the college. Central to the revival was a conviction that Jesus was the only way to salvation, creating an urgency for foreign missions. Soon after her conversion, Betsey expressed a desire to go to Africa as a missionary. This hope was not a viable option at the time because Betsey was unmarried. At this point in history, North American mission agencies had not sent out any single female missionaries to foreign lands. Even when they were sent out on missions in the United States, single women were required to go with a family for protection. There were also concerns the single female missionary might be taken advantage of, functioning as a "domestic servant or built-in babysitter" for the missionary family.[19] In addition, there were apprehensions that locals might assume the male missionary was keeping two wives. Just a few years after being freed from slavery, Betsey wanted to set aside her freedom in the United States to live in Africa as a missionary; however, these hopes could not be realized. She was single.

Fortunately, Betsey Stockton was not the only one who was catching missions vision during this time. Charles Stewart was a family friend of the Greens, frequently visiting Betsey's home. He desired to marry a woman named Harriet and move to the Sandwich Islands, which is now modern-day Hawaii.[20] With the protection of this family, Betsey could join them and now be able to serve as a missionary, just as she desired. However, the American Board of Commissioners for Foreign Missions (ABCFM) had to accept her. In order for this plan to come to fruition, multiple people had to advocate for Betsey's readiness to serve as a missionary. Dr. Green wrote a powerful letter to the mission board to recommend Betsey.[21] In addition, her teacher also wrote a letter of recommendation for her, stating,

> She has a larger acquaintance with sacred history and the Mosaic Institutions than almost any ordinary person, old or young I have ever known... I recollect a multitude of instances where, for my own information, I have questioned her about some fact in Biblical history, or some minute point in Jewish antiquities, and have immediately received a correct answer.[22]

Betsey knew she was ready to serve as a missionary. Before she could be commissioned, a special contract had to be written and agreed upon by the ABCFM, Betsey, Dr. Green, and the Stewarts.

The contract for Betsey seemed to be aimed at her protection, but it regarded her as separate and inferior to the other missionaries. It was not normal for missionaries to sign such a contract, but it was deemed necessary because of Betsey's situation as a single black female. In her contract, it was specified she was to be, "regarded and treated, neither as an equal nor as a servant, but as a humble Christian friend."[23] Betsey was also to be considered an assistant missionary. This had nothing to do with her race; it was solely based on her gender and education. Only ordained men could be considered full missionaries. All women, married or single, and non-ordained men had the status of "assistant missionary."[24] One key purpose of the document was to ensure Betsey's racial background and single status would not result in her being viewed as a domestic servant. Another purpose of the contract was to specify Betsey's relationship with the Stewart family. This revealed that the Stewart's were to protect Betsey, but also to clarify the boundaries of her role for the other missionaries.[25] Betsey was providing domestic help for the Stewart family, but she was not to be considered a servant for them or any other missionary. She was also expected to work as a teacher while on the island, so the contract clarified she needed to be able to fulfill those duties as well. These clarifications eventually proved necessary, as the Stewart family would later lean back on the contract to protect Betsey from mistreatment by other missionary families.

In 1822, Betsey Stockton became the first single female missionary to be sent from America to a foreign nation.[26] Betsey and the Stewart family sailed to the Sandwich Islands. From the start of their journey, it was clear the missionary life would be one filled with challenges and sacrifices. The first major challenge for the entire missionary group was the sea itself and battling the effects of seasickness. Betsey wrote it was "the most death-like sickness I ever felt in my life."[27] It was virtually impossible to sleep at night, as they were consistently thrown from their beds by the waves. During the day, it was challenging to stay standing without holding on to the boat, and the captain of the ship shared it was the worst conditions he had seen in his life. While Betsey was honest about the adverse living conditions of the boat, her sights were also set on more significant matters. She saw the connection between challenging physical realities and how they might influence spiritual health. She stated,

> I am glad to have it in my power to say, that notwithstanding our difficulties, I have never looked toward home with a longing eye... I am happy to tell you that since I left home, in all the stories and dangers I have been called to witness, I have never lost my self-possession. This I consider as a fulfillment the promise, that as my day is, so my strength shall be.[28]

In the face of physical sickness, lack of sleep, fear of thunderstorms, unclean water, and contaminated food, Betsey saw her spiritual battle as the most significant.

Throughout the journey on the ship and her time on the island, Betsey continuously monitored her spiritual health. She considered one of the greatest challenges on the ship to be the lack of a space to hide away to connect with God. Betsey wrote,

> Leaving home and becoming a missionary does not, I find, make peace with the great enemy—I find my heart, still inclined to forget God, and to wander in the paths of sin. We have no place in the ship to which we can retire, and spend a moment in secret with our God. This is one of my greatest privations: for the poor spark in my breast requires to be constantly fanned by prayer, to keep it from being extinguished. Sometimes I feel as though it were almost out.[29]

It was clear Betsey considered her connection to God to be of greater priority than her health and comfort, showing more concern over spiritual battles, than physical distresses.

After five months at sea, Betsey, the Stewarts, and the other missionary families finally landed safely on the Sandwich Islands. She found the natives to be pleasant people, but

FOR THE POOR SPARK IN MY BREAST REQUIRES TO BE CONSTANTLY FANNED BY PRAYER, TO KEEP IT FROM BEING EXTINGUISHED.

was surprised at how dirty they were and what foods they ate. Betsey was not impressed by the landscape, the society, the produce, or the sounds of the island. She found their language to be "most rude." [30] However, these were not issues of significance to her. Why? Her motivation for missions was simply obedience to the Lord. Betsey stated, "What then, you will say, are the charms which bind you to those islands? I answer, my duty, and the command of God."[31] Again, Betsey showed obedience to the Lord and her connection with Him was her highest value and motivation. She did not portray a false sense of spirituality while she served as a missionary or take pride in sacrifices she was making. Instead, she was honest regarding the struggles of remaining faithful:

You will be surprised if I tell you that it is much more difficult to keep the spirit alive here than it was at home. Oh, could Christians see us as we are struggling with the corruptions of our own hearts, and an overflowing torrent of pollution and guilt, they would soon learn to pray for us as they ought.[32]

During this time, Betsey grew very close to the Stewart family, but she also struggled with immense loneliness. She described her situation as, "without one friend with whom I can take sweet counsel, or a spot to which I can retire free from noise."[33] She continued to monitor her spiritual health, even to the point of wondering if she was truly saved. In her loneliness she stated, "I have serious doubts whether I ever passed from death unto life, and God has for wise reasons left me long, very long, in the dark, yet though cast down, He has not forgotten me."[34] Despite her doubts, she saw herself as an instrument in the Lord's hands. She saw clearly her purpose was to share the gospel with the people of the islands who did not yet know the Lord.

She spent much of her time ministering as a teacher. Betsey and some of the other missionaries moved to Lahaina (Maui) and began opening schools for locals. The first school was for the Hawaiian chiefs and their families; however, they quickly began to open more schools for the rest of the population. Eventually, Betsey was responsible for the first school on the island that was aimed at educating farmers. She was an excellent teacher and quickly acquired the local language. She spent much of her time teaching those who were not previously given access to education, a striking reflection of the opportunities she was given as a young girl. In 1825, the poor health of Harriet Stewart led the family and Betsey to leave the island and return to the United States.

Upon returning, Betsey continued to educate others and mobilize them to engage in mission work. She stayed connected to the Stewart family, helping care for the children for many years. She remained with them even after Harriet died. Consistently overcoming loneliness, she would persevere. She went on to start a public school for black children.[35] She later helped establish the Witherspoon Street Presbyterian Church and helped start a school where she taught for many years.

Betsey Stockton died in 1865 in Princeton. The president of the university conducted her funeral.

Betsey Stockton was indeed a trailblazer. The first single female missionary sent from America, a former slave, and an educator who had received no formal education herself. She was beloved, and yet she experienced depths of loneliness that are nearly impossible to fathom. Through it all, Betsey was driven by obedience to the Lord and was focused on abiding in Him as her source of strength. She desperately relied on prayer and was honest about her weaknesses. She forged a path for generations of women to follow, one of bold obedience to Christ, dedication to His heart for the world, unwavering authenticity, and perseverance.

Here I Am God, Send My Sister.

LOTTIE MOON

A Feisty Foreign Devil
By Caroline Studdard

Picture the girl you know who you feel would be least likely to be a missionary. Is there one who comes to mind who is indifferent toward missions—even mocks Christianity entirely? This was Lottie Moon. The feistiness that kept her from God's kingdom went on to become her greatest asset. It kept her on the field as a missionary and helped her to pioneer the way for countless women to join in giving up their lives for the sake of gospel.

Lottie Moon was born into a life of privilege and status. She was the daughter of a wealthy plantation owner and had the benefit of higher education in a time when parents were cautioned about educating their girls. Society claimed overeducated women could be "dangerous." If that was the case, then Lottie was one of the most dangerous women in the South.

Charlotte Digges "Lottie" Moon, was born December 12, 1840, in Virginia and grew up in the town of Viewmont. Lottie and her siblings spent their days running around their father's plantation and learning the ways of being "proper Southern children." Lottie had all of the clothing, entertainment, and education she could dream of. Lottie's parents, Anna and Edward Moon, made sure each of their seven children were educated and brought up in the best and proper society.

Every Sunday, the children would dedicate themselves to reading the Bible and other Christian books that were morally uplifting and fitting for the Christian life. They read biographies of missionaries like Ann Judson, who traveled to Burma to share her faith. However, Lottie would have rather been outside climbing trees and chasing her siblings.

She always had a knack for playing, particularly playing jokes on people. When Lottie was in school at Hollins Institute, on the eve of April Fool's Day 1856, she snuck out of her dorm room in the middle of the night, her bed sheets in hand, and climbed into the rafters where the school bell was kept. She wound her sheets around the large metal bell again and again and secured the sheets with rope. The next morning no bell rang to rouse the young ladies from their beds. They all woke up slowly and late, which caused a panic among the students. Lottie could hardly control her glee—but her sheet-less bed soon gave her away.

Lottie enjoyed her pranks and her friends, but she was also a dedicated student. She went on to study French and Latin. She ultimately received her masters of arts from the Albemarle Female Institute, the female counterpart to the University of Virginia. She was among the first five women in the South to do so and was at the top of her class. Lottie was declared the "most educated woman in the South."[36]

During this time the women's rights movement was in full swing. Lottie was passionate about championing the rights of women in education and in the public sphere. Despite her upbringing, Lottie did not see how the church or Christianity could fit into the movement. The church she knew seemed to stifle women, not support them. During her time at Albemarle she considered the idea of following Christ. However, she soon decided her middle initial "D" stood for "Devil" instead. Just like the feisty devil she was, Lottie

would argue and debate anyone who spoke to her about Christianity. One night after she had attended a church service with her classmates, she began to examine her own heart. She began to think through her arguments on why she was not a Christian. Were her views sound, or had her view of Christianity been poisoned by her peers?

After much internal debate, Lottie made a life-changing decision. She decided to follow Christ! The next morning she walked into one of the prayer meetings to make her declaration to her classmates. One of the girls exclaimed, "Lottie Moon thinks she's too clever to become a Christian; she's just here to stir up trouble." [37] Fortunately, this time eighteen-year-old Lottie was serious.

After graduation, Lottie returned home to help her family face the tide of Civil War. The Moons lost much land and money, and their family life would never be the same. Lottie and her siblings fought hard to make use of their talents and time during the war and to face the aftermath it caused.

After the war, Lottie's passion for education took her to Kentucky, Virginia, and Georgia to teach. It was while teaching in Kentucky Lottie learned of the needs of China.

She heard Dr. George Burton speak about his time as a missionary in China. Lottie was mesmerized by all he had to say. It struck her that a group of people on the other side of the globe had never heard the name of Christ or the message of the Gospel. She was intrigued by the idea she could be the one to go and tell them. Yet how would she get to China? She was a single woman.

The road to China opened up for Lottie in an unexpected way—through her youngest sister, Edmonia. On April 16, 1872, Lottie received a shocking letter from Edmonia, or Eddie, as her family called her. She had managed to get herself appointed to be a missionary to China! Edmonia petitioned the mission board to send her as a single missionary to be a part of a married team on the field, and the board agreed! Edmonia "Eddie" Moon was the first single female missionary to be sent to China, and her older sister Lottie would soon join her.

The Moon sisters' decision to go and serve the Chinese people was not typical for women of their education, family background, and social position. Their love of their heavenly Father compelled them to go to the Chinese people who had never heard the name of Jesus. Lottie said in a letter to the mission board before she left,

> Could a Christian woman possibly desire a higher honor than to be permitted to go from house to house and tell of a Savior to those who have never heard His name? We could not conceive a life which would more thoroughly satisfy the mind and heart of a true follower of the Lord Jesus.[38]

The mission board approved Lottie to join her sister in China, and on October 7, 1873, when Lottie was thirty-two-years-old, she set foot on Chinese soil. Her team consisted of a young widow Sallie Holmes, a married couple, Tarleton and Martha Crawford, and her sister.

Since she had mastered languages in school, Lottie felt confident she could pick up the Chinese language quickly; however, it would not be as simple as she imagined. Mandarin, one of the main Chinese languages, is a tonal language, which meant if the same sounds were made at a higher or lower pitch, the meaning of the word would change — sometimes drastically. In addition to Mandarin, Lottie would need to learn the many different dialects that were spoken around the area of Tengchow, the village where she lived. Lottie was a long way from her Southern-belle roots, but she was confident God was with her.

Lottie's primary objective in Tengchow was to help teach and start a school. However, her passion was sharing the gospel with the villagers—specifically the women. Lottie wrote in a letter to the mission board,

> ...Women, too, may find [a place on the mission field]. In city and in village, thousands of women will never hear the gospel until women bear it to them. They will admit women, but men cannot gain access to their homes, nor will they come to church. The only way for them to hear the good news of salvation is from the lips of foreign women. Are there not some, yeah many, who find it in their hearts to say, "Here am I, send me?"[39]

The work was not picturesque or easy. One evening, Lottie and her teammate Sallie wandered into the chilling rain to share the gospel with a group of villagers who had requested they come.

When they arrived dripping wet, the people pleaded with them to share and teach them from the "heavenly book." Lottie was happy, but as she attempted to warm herself in the small hut, she realized this was more difficult than she could have ever imagined. People were constantly staring at her, touching her, talking to her in a new language; but she was determined to conquer her unwillingness and discomfort to spread the good news of the gospel.

Lottie later wrote to Dr. Henry Tupper, secretary of the Southern Baptist Convention's Foreign Mission Board, to confess her struggle with the physical and mental hardships of missionary life:

> I am always ashamed to dwell on physical hardships. But, this time I have departed from my usual reticence because I know that there are some who, in their pleasant homes in America without any real knowledge of the facts, declare that the days of missionary hardships are over. To speak in the open air in a foreign tongue from six to eleven times a day is no trifle. The fatigue of trail is something... If anyone fancies sleeping on brick beds in rooms with dirt floors and walls blackened by the smoke of many generations... and the stable itself being within three feet of your door, I wish to declare most emphatically that as a matter of taste, I differ... I find it most unpleasant. If anyone thinks that the constant risk of exposure to smallpox and other contagious disease, against which the Chinese take no precaution whatsoever, is just the most charming thing in life, I shall continue to differ. In a word, let him try it! A few days of roughing it as we ladies do habitually will convince the most skeptical.[40]

Lottie labored in tough conditions for the love of her Savior. She was not shy about the realities of life on the field; in fact she was exact and direct with people who wished to come and serve in China.

In a letter to Annie Armstrong, the leader of the Women's Missionary Union, Lottie encouraged her to send new missionaries to China, but she did not mince words about the reality of life on the field:

> Say to the new missionaries that they are coming to a life of hardship, responsibility, and constant self-denial. They must live, the greater part of the time, in a Chinese house, in close contact with the people. They will be alone in the interior and will need to be strong and courageous. If the joy of the Lord be their strength, the blessedness of the work will more than compensate for its hardships. Let them come rejoicing to suffer for the sake of that Lord and Master who freely gave His life for them.[41]

Lottie rejoiced to suffer for her Savior. After years working in Tengchow, she relocated to a village called P'ingtu. She was pioneering in areas where the gospel had never been proclaimed. She moved into a Chinese-style home and adopted Chinese dress, at first for warmth during the cold winters, but then she found the villagers did not jeer or stare as often when she wore their clothes.

> SAY TO THE NEW MISSIONARIES THAT THEY ARE COMING TO A LIFE OF HARDSHIP, RESPONSIBILITY AND CONSTANT SELF-DENIAL.

Her dedication and creativity to reach the Chinese people are inspiring and encouraging. She had a fire in her heart to proclaim the name of Christ. It was her love of Christ and His gospel that propelled her forward in times of stress and confusion. Many people feared and rejected Lottie, but as any good Southern woman knows, a meal can entice visitors. The people did not immediately run to Lottie for cookies, but slowly, the children came and ate; and, slowly, the mothers came and ate and stayed to talk. Then the leaders of the village came. Soon the people of P'ingtu had adopted Lottie. Eventually, many went on to accept Christ. The need in fact was so great Lottie sent for more missionaries from Tengchow to come and teach the new believers in P'ingtu.

Lottie was a pioneer in missions by living with the people she served and adopting their culture. Typically, missionaries from the West would build compounds and live in a western setting with all of their comforts and provisions while ministering to locals. Lottie made little to no progress with the villagers while she retained her western dress and customs. She decided she could make a deeper impact if she gave up western comforts and moved from an urban center to rural China. As she moved closer to the local people and lived life more in tune with their customs and culture, things were not immediately easier, however.

IF THE JOY OF THE LORD BE THEIR STRENGTH, THE BLESSEDNESS OF THE WORK WILL MORE THAN COMPENSATE FOR ITS HARDSHIPS.

Lottie lived a life of hardship. She entered into a life of poverty and rejection in the name of Christ. His joy and His grace sustained her in the midst of daily life. She soldiered on—not for her own renown, but for the Lord's name and for the joy and the salvation of her beloved Chinese.

While living in P'ingtu, some of the villagers woke her up in the middle of the night. They begged her to come and help one of her friends and new believers, Dan Ho-bang. He was being beaten for his faith. She rose quickly and went with them. When she arrived, Ho-bang was tied up and the leader of the mob was prepared to kill him if he did not renounce Christ. Lottie, who was a small woman, under 5-feet-tall, stepped in front of the leader and did something unbelievable! She said, "If you try to destroy the church here, and the Christians who worship in it, you will have to kill me first. Our Master, Jesus, gave His life for us Christians, and now I am ready to die for Him."[42] The leader of the mob went to strike Lottie with his sword, but it inexplicably dropped from his hands and fell to the ground. The mob realized the power of God, and they dared not fight one of his followers. Slowly, the mob dispersed, and Lottie and her friends began praising God.

Lottie served in China almost forty years. She watched her sister and multiple teammates suffer from physical and emotional distress, and as a result, return back to the United States. In 1912, at the insistence of her team and the mission board, Lottie was sent to the United States to recover her health. She died Christmas Eve 1912, on the journey across the Pacific Ocean. She was seventy-two years old.

Lottie was passionate about raising up workers and awakening the church. Her love for the Chinese people carried over into her bold and consistent pleas via letters. She did not downplay what life would be like on the field.

In Lottie's now famous letter to the Foreign Mission Journal she rouses the church, specifically women, to commit to the vision of Christ to support His church and His mission around the globe. She wrote on September 15, 1887:

> ...instead of the paltry offerings we make, do something that will prove that we are really in earnest in claiming to be followers of Him who, though He was rich, for our sake became poor?... The rising of the tide [in sending missionaries]

seems to have begun with the enlisting of the women of the church in the cause of missions.

How many there are among our women who imagine that because Jesus paid it all, they need pay nothing, forgetting the prime object of their salvation was that they should follow in the footsteps of Jesus Christ in bringing back a lost world to God, and so aid in bringing the answer to the petition our Lord taught His disciples: "Thy kingdom come." [43]

Those words ring as true today as they did over one-hundred-years-ago. Will we give our lives to the King we follow, or will we turn our eye from the commands He has given us His daughters? Will we serve our King, or will we serve ourselves?

AMY CARMICHAEL

Daring Mother to Many
By Sara Bauer

Being a risk taker can be a polarizing thing. There is part of us that wants to have that kind of courage, but there's no shortage of voices, including our own, to talk us out of it. For Amy Carmichael, no voice was louder than the Lord's, and His authority in her life led her into risks so many people thought were foolish. Now looking back, no one can deny they were risks worth taking.

In the tenth century, a kinsman of the King of Scotland was hanged by an enemy. Upon hearing this news, King Kenneth II offered a large reward to any subject who would dare remove the body and return it to him. One stepped forward and said simply, "dal ziel," or "I dare" in Gaelic. Afterward, "Dalziel" became his name.[44] The same courageous, valiant spirit was passed down centuries later to his great-great-granddaughter, Amy Wilson Carmichael. Amy was a woman who held

40

unswervingly to her convictions: in the face of extreme situations, disapproval from others, and danger, she desired to complete the mission God had given her in each season of her life. Amy dared to be different for the sake of the eternal.

Amy was born December 16, 1867, in the coastal Irish village of Millisle. The Carmichael family managed the local flour mill, and their home was filled with laughter, conviction, and love.

Describing her childhood, Amy said "I don't think there could have been a happier child than I was."[45] That was, until the unexpected death of her father at the age of 17. This plunged the family into a financial crisis and Amy into the responsibility of helping to raise her six brothers and sisters. This would be the first of many obstacles Amy would face that would define her purpose and draw her closer to her God.

It wasn't long after the death of her father Amy had the first decisive moment that changed the direction of her life.[46] On their way to church, Amy and her family encountered an older woman carrying a heavy bundle of rags. She and her brothers stepped in to help her, and immediately felt the judgement from the "proper church ladies" as they passed on their way to church. The stark divide between the church and the poor before her hit Amy. She saw how much the church focused on appearances while neglecting opportunities to show God's love to those hurting around them. It was then she heard the words of Paul the Apostle, "Gold, silver, precious stones, wood, hay, stubble. If any man's work abides..." (1 Corinthians 3:12-13). She spent time that afternoon pondering what she was building in her life that would last for eternity. God was slowly opening the heart of a teenager whose life He had appointed to touch the lives of thousands.

A significant influence in her life was the Keswick conventions. These were gatherings designed to promote total devotion to God in Europe.[47] She attended her first in 1886, and it opened her eyes to see her life and the world in light of eternity. At her first convention, she was amazed at the thought that God is able to keep us from falling. Amy was pondering this thought at lunch, and noticed her friend send back undercooked mutton chops. She thought to herself, "What does it matter about mutton chops? The Lord is able to keep us from falling!"[48] She was beginning to see the weight of God's mission and the insignificance of earthly cares. She saw this as the measure of her commitment to her Savior and staking her all on the eternally significant. Instead of being distracted by the temporal, she became enamored with knowing God deeper and joining Him in however He led her.

Amy returned home and immediately saw an opportunity. She recognized the poor children and women of the neighborhoods were often neglected. She set out to begin Bible studies in their community. Nearly every day, multiple times a day, she was teaching or interacting with her friends from the slums. She started a program called the "Morning Watch" to encourage them to read the Bible daily. This grew to over 500, and she realized they needed their own building. Amy started praying for God to provide, and soon an older woman heard of her ministry and offered to pay the bill for an entire aluminum hall to be built. Realizing she needed land, Amy marched straight to the owner of the biggest mill in the city and daringly asked what he would charge for a piece of land. He sold it for a small price, and they built a building she named "The Welcome." As her ministry grew, she realized she needed help. She prayed, and the Lord provided more volunteers for The Welcome. Word of her success spread, and she was asked to launch a similar ministry in Manchester, England, in 1889.

As her ministry grew, she continued to return to the Keswick conventions to sharpen and renew her vision. When hearing Hudson Taylor speak about the four thousand who die every hour without hearing the gospel, she was gripped. Amy wrote in a journal,

> Does it not stir up our hearts, to go forth and help
> them, does it not make us long to leave our luxury,
> our exceeding abundant light, and go to them that
> sit in darkness?[49]

She pleaded with the Lord that week for rest from the "cry of the heathen" that haunted her. Ironically, the thought that God might call her to go to them did not enter her mind.

During this time she met an older gentlemen named Mr. Wilson. They were soon good friends, and he became an adoptive father to her. She began calling him the DOM (dear old man). Amy lived with the DOM and his family, and this season of her life was marked by growth in knowledge of God and the Bible. She loved them dearly and decided to take "Wilson" as her own name, changing her name to "Amy Wilson Carmichael." She grew to appreciate the many ways of Christian worship as she attended an Anglican church with the DOM (though she grew up Presbyterian). She also greatly enjoyed deep, theological discussions with the DOM. Little did they know what this time of spiritual growth was preparing her for.

Amy often took note of many spiritual milestones throughout her life. One of the greatest happened on January 13, 1892. On that snowy evening she heard, "Go ye," and immediately knew she had to go to the unreached. Though it was a sobering and weighty call, she couldn't ignore this clear command.

Her first thought was what her mother might say. She wrote a beautiful letter explaining her heart,

> My precious mother, have you given your child unreservedly to the Lord for whatever He wills? O may He strengthen you to say yes to Him if He asks something which costs.[50]

To her surprise, Amy's mother responded with,

> He (Jesus) is yours—you are His—to take you where He pleases and to use you as He pleases. I can trust you to Him and I do... All day He has helped me, and my heart unfailingly says, "Go ye."[51]

The DOM responded in a similar way: "It was the Lord who asked of her. Who could say no?"[52] Amy had the earthly support and encouragement she longed for. However, there were many other voices who disagreed. This truly hurt Amy. A doctor refused to give her permission to go. Others called her foolish. That didn't stop her daring spirit. She was on a mission. She set sail to Japan in autumn of 1892 as the first Keswick-funded missionary.

O MAY HE STRENGTHEN YOU TO SAY YES TO HIM IF HE ASKS SOMETHING WHICH COSTS.

Goodbyes were tearful, but the hardest was with the DOM. On the dock, they comforted each other with Scripture. As the ship sailed away, the entire crowd both on board and on the dock joined in a chorus of *"Crown Him with Many Crowns"* and *"Like a River Glorious is God's Perfect Peace."* In Amy's generation of launching missionaries, the goodbyes were much more permanent. There was a greater chance it could be an earthly goodbye as well. Not wanting to waste the time she had on the ship, she began Bible studies and services for sailors. It must have been a funny-looking group: Amy, a young woman from Ireland and a bunch of rough African and Asian sailors. By the end of her studies with them, several had made professions of faith and even signed a promise to quit drinking alcohol. Amy dared to build on the eternal in whatever season the Lord put her in.

AMY DARED TO BUILD ON THE ETERNAL IN WHATEVER SEASON THE LORD PUT HER IN.

Five months later, Amy landed in Japan. With the zeal of a new missionary, she dove into ministry. After a few months the hardships began. She was excited to have a team to work with; however, their philosophy of ministry was different. She longed to change her dress, schedule, and diet to better relate with the Japanese women she was reaching, but her team was resistant to the changes. She persisted in her challenge to dress and eat like the Japanese. She did gain permission to wear a Japanese kimono, and a few of her teammates followed in her example.

Unlike most missionaries who write about the successes on the field, Amy was constantly recognizing and sharing how difficult the mission field was. She wrote,

> It is more important that you should know about the reverses than about the success of the war... We shall have all eternity to celebrate the victories, but we have only the few hours before sunset in which to win them... So we have tried to tell you the truth—the uninteresting, unromantic truth.[53]

The struggle with loneliness in singleness hit her hard d
her first year in Japan. Years later, she recounts one instance
where she retreated to a cave to wrestle with God about it:

> On this day many years ago I went away alone to a cave
> in the mountain called Arima. I had feelings of fear
> about the future. That was why I went there—to be
> alone with God. The devil kept on whispering, "It's all
> right now, but what about afterwards? You are going to
> be very lonely." And he painted pictures of loneliness. I
> can see them still. And I turned to my God in a kind of
> desperation and said, "Lord, what can I do? How can I
> go on to the end?" And He said, "None of them that
> trust in Me shall be desolate." That word has been with
> me ever since. It has been fulfilled to me. It will be
> fulfilled to you.[54]

She was silent about her own singleness, though she actively
took part in encouraging others to pursue the role God was
calling them to. In her journals, we only see two instances
where marriage, or what she called "the other life," seemed to
be a possibility. She never mentioned who. It was clear a
proposal had to have been made. Amy was committed not to
settle and instead live a life completely surrendered to Jesus.
She clung to the words of 1 Corinthians 7:34, "The unmarried
woman careth for the things of the Lord, that she may be holy
both in body and in spirit." She did not see her calling to
singleness as more elite than the married woman. Instead she
wrote,

> Remember our God did not say to me, "I have
> something greater for you to do." This life is not
> greater than the other, but it is different. That is all. For
> some our Father chooses one, for some He chooses the
> other, all that matters is that we should be obedient
> "unto all meeting of His wishes."[55]

46

Another obstacle to holiness Amy found was the sinfulness of herself. Elisabeth Elliott in her book *A Chance to Die* writes,

> She was finding firsthand that missionaries are not set apart from the rest of the human race, not purer, nobler, higher. "Wings are an illusive fallacy," she wrote. "Some may possess them, but they are not very visible, and as for me, there isn't the least sign of a feather. Don't imagine that by crossing the sea and landing on a foreign shore and learning a foreign lingo you 'burst the bonds of outer sin and hatch yourself a cherubim.'"[56]

FOR SOME OUR FATHER CHOOSES ONE, FOR SOME HE CHOOSES THE OTHER, ALL THAT MATTERS IS THAT WE SHOULD BE OBEDIENT UNTO ALL MEETING OF HIS WISHES.

She consistently pleaded for those at home to pray. Her greatest desire was holiness. Later in her life, Sherwood Eddy, a missionary author, writes about her character,

Here is the point where many a missionary breaks down. Every normal missionary sails with high purpose but as a very imperfect Christian. His character is his weakest point. But Amy Wilson Carmichael was the most Christ-like character I had ever met, and her life was the most fragrant, the most joyfully sacrificial, that I ever knew.[57]

Like Paul, her hardships were many. She began struggling with her health, and was forced to leave Japan and go to Ceylon (modern-day Sri Lanka). Amy was sensitive to the Lord's leading, and was immediately obedient, even if she hadn't asked others permission. Direction came to her in three ways:

through Scripture, the leading of the Spirit, and changing circumstances.

Once again, Amy set to work sharing the gospel with the Buddhist people in Ceylon. She began visiting Buddhist priests directly to talk of spiritual things and take questions from them about Christianity. Everything seemed to be lining up for her to begin a work in Ceylon permanently, until she received devastating news. The DOM had had a stroke. She was summoned back to England immediately.

Amy spent the next ten months in England spending time with the DOM before his death. It was also a time for her to regain her health and mobilize others to the mission. The doctors told her she could not return to a tropical climate, so she began looking for a new location. A friend wrote to her about India. She applied and was accepted to a missionary society who would send her. Nothing would deter Amy from the mission God had called her to. She delivered a farewell address at her home church before she went. "Who can forget," wrote a clergyman, "Miss Amy Wilson Carmichael's farewell address, where she left for her life of sacrifice in India, as she unrolled a 'ribbon of blue' with the golden words, 'Nothing too precious for Jesus.'"[58]

This was the last time Amy would see Europe.

Arriving in India, she was appalled by the vast amount of idol worship. Looking out across a crowded marketplace at the flood of people with the Hindu god Shiva's ashes on their foreheads, she said, "It makes you feel as if you couldn't sit still. You must do something, try to do something, anything!"[59] The hold the enemy had on Indians through idol worship angered her. She passionately engaged in the spiritual battle for the souls of the Indians she was growing to love. Once Amy rang a bell to gather the servants for prayers. A boy pointed to the bell and mischievously said, "It's a god." Sure enough, it had a scratched face on the handle. Amy immediately knocked the bell handle off and pushed it into a nearby fire. Another time, she and her friend Saral discovered three stones under a tree. They were idols. She recalled,

> To see those stupid stones standing there to the honor of the false gods, in the midst of the true God's beauty was too much for us. We knocked them over and down they crashed and over they rolled forwith. Oh the shame of it! It makes one burn to think of His glory being given to another.[60]

Her most moving perspective of the desperate state of the unreached came through a dream. She wrote about this dream in her book, *Things As They Are*. She described watching in horror as blind people stumble off of a cliff with no one to warn them. She noticed groups of people who can see, sitting together making daisy chains and ignoring those walking hopelessly off the edge. She wondered why these people sitting there making flower necklaces would not stand up and help those falling into the darkness. This dream haunted Amy throughout her life.

Upon arriving in India, Amy engaged in Tamil language study with the Walkers, another missionary family. Thomas Walker encouraged her to pursue more difficult pieces of literature: poems and Tamil classics. Naturally, Amy chose the harder route. Soon she was able to share her first Bible story without the help of a translator. After her time studying, Walker saw much promise in Amy and asked if she would partner with him in their village work. She accepted. They traveled from village to village, handing out Bibles and sharing stories with anyone who would listen.

Amy asked God for faithful friends to join in her ministry. God answered her through several Indian Christian women. They called themselves the "Starry Cluster." Her desire was true discipleship. She wanted to train them to embrace the uttermost love, which meant uttermost obedience to their King. She taught them English so they could take part in the spiritual riches she had found in her favorite books. After their study, they vowed together to love their Savior above all else.

Amy's favorite pastime was writing. No matter how busy she was, she found time to write about her experiences and prioritized mobilizing the church back home.

She was always attempting to call people to obedience in mission, but also share the realities of the hardships awaiting them on the field. She wrote a book specifically about how difficult India was. The publisher refused to print it, saying it would deter people from missions. Amy sent it back, simply changing the name of the book to *Things As They Are*. This book created a stir back home, even inspiring a group of Indian missionaries to ask the mission society if they would send Amy back to England because of the interest her book created.

In 1901 Amy moved to a town called Dohnavur. Amy observed a Hindu temple and noticed children enslaved there. Little girls were often given to the temple to be "married to the gods" and would become their slaves. Amy became known as "the child-stealing mother."[61] A seven-year-old girl named Preena was given by her mother to the temple for service. After several attempts, she managed to escape and set out to find Amy. When she found Amy, Preena immediately ran up, sat on her lap, and began calling her "Amma," or "mother". It was from Preena that Amy learned firsthand of the true condition of the temple. The children were sex slaves for the priests. Amy had to respond. She began searching for more children to rescue from this darkness.

Amy struggled with her new role as mother to these girls. She started recruiting others around her to help rescue children. Many missionaries and Indian locals were indifferent. Finally, a few pastors began to help her rescue children. By 1904, they had 17 children.

Amy had found her calling. Another blessing arrived later that year: her mother came for a visit, just in time for Christmas. Mrs. Carmichael wrote to a friend about Amy's life in India,

> An atmosphere of love and obedience pervades the compound... A set of more loving, unselfish women and girls and children could not easily be found... Since we came here a month ago I can truthfully say [Amy] has scarcely had leisure even to eat. She is mother, doctor, and nurse, day and night.[62]

Though much joy was found in her ministry, there was much hardship as well. Deadly disease attacked the children in the compound. An epidemic struck and took the lives of three of the babies. It was painful to lose the children she loved, but Amy knew she was entrusting them to their loving Father. Amy wrote this poem for Indraneela, a baby girl who died:

Dear little feet so eager to be walking—
　　But never walked in any grieving way,
Dear little mouth, so eager to be talking—
　　But never hurt with words it learned to say;
Dear little hands, outstretched in eager welcome,
　　Dear little head, that close against me lay—
Father, to Thee I give my Indraneela;
　　Thou wilt take care of her until That Day.[63]

The ministry was growing. The enemy's pressure was real. Ten more babies died.

Several of those closest to her suddenly died: her beloved friend and fellow worker Ponnammal, and then Mr. Walker. Then Amy received word her own mother died as well. The pain was immense. Elisabeth Elliot writes of her perseverance and perspective through it,

> "Naturally, there was some pressure"—the understatement of the year, encompassing the thousand anxieties of the huge responsibility, the what ifs, the buts, the whys, the help-Thou-mine-unbeliefs. She had to live in the middle of this, to go on making decisions, leading the prayer meetings, writing her letters and her books and her journals, bearing on her mind and in her prayers the name of each individual... When the disciples returned from their apostolic travels, the Lord asked them, "Did you lack anything?" Their answer was, "Nothing." Would Amy Carmichael give any other answer? She would not. [64]

One distinctive about Amy's method of ministry was her philosophy of fundraising. She strongly believed a missionary should not ask for money, but simply ask God and trust Him to provide. Time after time, she records stories of God providing very specifically at just the right time. As Dohnavur grew, they needed more space and facilities, medical care, and food for the children. God provided every need. Her position was always, "Our Heavenly Father knows what we need and gives it to us."[65] This was again tested when their ministry began to expand.

Amy discovered the slavery epidemic in Hindu temples was not limited to girls. Boys were also sold. She immediately began investigating—learning where they lived, what their daily activity looked like, and most importantly how she could rescue them. Others at Dohnavur questioned her bringing boys into their care, pointing out she would need new facilities, male workers, and restructuring of their existing ministry. She politely listened, but believed God had given her a divine responsibility. Burdened with this opportunity, she sought God in the woods one afternoon, asking Him to either take away her burden for the boys or show her how to act. God affirmed her desire, and she began making a plan for action. Amy always moved toward the impossible task God called her to.

Amy drew up the plans for a new building and prayed for the amount needed to cover the cost. On the very next mail day, they received a donation for the exact amount! It was difficult to rescue boys, but they finally received their first, Arul. By 1926, they had eighty boys at Dohnavur. The need for men in the ministry was even more immediate, but it was difficult to convince men to join the work. Amy persistently prayed for more men, and specifically a doctor, to join the fellowship. Again God answered. A doctor and teacher moved to Dohnavur. Immediately plans were made for a hospital, and the missionaries began asking God for the money. God provided. The hospital was built, and the fellowship continued to grow.

Word about Amy's ministry began spreading in Europe. Many were mobilized to pray and some even sailed to join her. She was passionate about preparing and screening missionary candidates for the work, and created twenty-five questions she asked every individual who came to help. Though her ministry continued to grow, she held firm to the same principles of integrity, love for God, and realness.

Amy found it difficult to answer the specific questions the missionary societies asked about her plans for ministry and measurement of success. She was blazing her own trail in ministry, and that left the societies at a loss on how to support her. In 1927 the Dohnavur Fellowship registered as their own organization. Their mission was simple:

To save children in moral danger, to train them to serve others; to succor the desolate and the suffering; to do anything that may be shown to the will of our Heavenly Father, in order to make His love known, especially to the people of India.[66]

By the beginning of the 1930's, the years of hard work were beginning to hold Amy back from her vigor of ministry. Her health was deteriorating, and she began to see the need to appoint others to lead. An increasingly limited capacity tempted Amy to be disappointed, but she continued to see her weakness as an opportunity for God to provide strength. Then, the unimaginable happened. Amy experienced a horrific injury. She fell and twisted her spine. She was bedridden for the next fifteen years!

Amy would not let her limitations keep her from obedience and continued to minister to people through writing. She penned thirty-seven books. When she lost the use of her right hand, she still continued writing with the help of a scribe.

Those closest to her remember, though she was most tempted, she never complained about what God chose to do, or not do, even during the trying time of confinement. She kept many verses and hymns near her bedside to comfort her in the darkness. A thin brass Celtic cross lay on her nightstand that read, "In this sign conquer." Still the daring faith and courage of her fore fathers lived on in eighty-year-old Amy as she quietly reminded herself to keep on conquering by the power of her Lord's cross even while bedridden.

In January 1951 she fell into a coma. The nearly 900 members of the Dohnavur Fellowship came to visit and say goodbye. Then, on January 18, at age eighty-three, she passed away in her sleep, as she always believed the Lord would take her. They laid her to rest under a tree at Donhavur fellowship. Her tombstone was a small simple bird bath with one word inscribed on it: "Amma," or mother. Amy, the bold, loving, zealous single woman from Ireland continues to be remembered as the mother of thousands in India.

Those who knew her remember her love and acceptance of people. Amy was a combination of stern and steeled, set out to do the will of God despite all obstacles, yet a tender-hearted and loving mother to everyone around her. In the words of Elisabeth Elliot, "Her life is another case in point of how grace goes to work on the raw material of individual nature."[67] The many daring risks Amy took, which seemed foolish to those around her, resulted in a vast spiritual influence greater than she could have ever imagined.

Today the Dohnavur Fellowship continues to serve children in India. To date, 2,000 girls and 700 boys have been rescued and live in the fellowship. There is also an active hospital, which sees 40,000 patients each year.[68] Will the school and hospital last forever? No. But God knows the spiritual work He accomplished through the bold, joyful sacrifice of Amy Wilson Carmichael. If Amy could encourage us today, she would certainly call us out of the ordinary and into great risk for the sake of the Cross. She would dare us to do everything we can to know and love God to the deepest point possible, which she believed would drive us to conquer the impossible in His name. Amy's life proved it is worth it to give up the earthly desires to long for something greater: the joy of complete surrender. This may seem like a daring move, but is the only way to pursue something so much more meaningful and satisfying: God using a human life to glorify Himself among the nations.

BERTHA CONDE

Mobilizer on a Mission
By Taylor Marie

Have you ever asked the question, "What is God's will for my life?" or wondered if you're doing the thing He truly wants you to be doing with your talents, gifts, and resources? Bertha Conde is an example of a woman who kept a close ear to what God was calling her to—and placed priority on His plans above her own.

Bertha Conde took on many roles in her life. She was an author, world traveler, inspirational speaker, a pastor; but her most important role was that of a mobilizer. Bertha's devotion to see Christ made known among all the peoples of the world was electrifying. She was a bold woman who followed a big God and she knew He had big plans for the world. Wherever she went and whatever she did she sought to play a role in His grand story.

Bertha Conde was born on November 27, 1871, in Auburn, New York, where she lived with her parents and two sisters. As a young adult, she attended Smith College in Massachusetts and graduated in 1895 with her bachelor's degree in Natural Sciences. After graduating, she attended Free Church College in Glasgow, Scotland, where she studied theology. When she

56

returned to the United States, Bertha became a professor at Elmira College in New York.[69] After two years she began serving at the Christadora Settlement House, where she helped provide healthcare, education, and job training, along with other services to poor immigrant families.

In 1898, Bertha met a young woman named Ruth Rouse. Ruth worked for an organization called the Student Christian

Movement (SCM). Ruth and others in SCM helped to mobilize both men and women to serve as missionaries. Ruth saw great potential in Bertha and recruited her to work alongside her as a mobilizer with the SCM. Bertha's passion for God and her love for others set her on a path to be a life-long mobilizer. She encouraged university students from all around the world to go and serve the nations.

Bertha gave her life to see women and men alike rise up as followers of Christ to further the movement of the gospel and the growth of the church. More specifically, Bertha sought to empower women to step out of their fears: fear of singleness, fear of leaving their roles within the household, fear of becoming sick or ill, and even fear of losing their lives.[70] She helped women see God's plan and the opportunity He extended to each of them to step out in faith and watch Him do a mighty work in and through their lives.

When Bertha looked at the heart of God for women in the church and what was happening in the world, she saw a disconnect. God created women, like men, to be His image bearers (Genesis 1:27). Jesus' heart was for men *and* women to be a part of His global plan. Jesus gave women status within a society that sought to oppress them. Throughout history, wherever Jesus is shared and accepted, the social, legal, and spiritual status of women rises.[71]

As a single woman in a time when women were not allowed to vote, Bertha was publishing books about discipleship, evangelism, and friendship. She was determined to follow Christ even if it meant going against the cultural social norms of her time. She attended a graduate school of theology, supported the women's suffrage movement, served as an executive member for the Young Women's Christian Association, and was one of the longest running executive members for the Student Volunteer Movement for Foreign Missions (SVMFM). As a member of the SVMFM, she spoke to men and women all over the world. She traveled to twenty-seven countries, and her lectures exhorted communities to provide opportunities for women to be educated and included in church communities.[72] She knew the church as a whole could only flourish the way it was designed to if both men and women played their part to take the gospel where it was not preached.

> **THROUGHOUT HISTORY, WHEREVER JESUS IS SHARED AND ACCEPTED, THE SOCIAL, LEGAL, AND SPIRITUAL STATUS OF WOMEN RISES.**

She was a woman of prayer. Like Christ commanded His disciples in Matthew 9:38, Bertha prayed. She prayed without ceasing for God to raise up laborers for His glory and to send them out into the world so others could come to know Him, so that the whole world would be "filled with the glory and the knowledge of the Lord..." (Habakkuk 2:14).

During the time Bertha was on the SVMFM, the executive committee spoke on the topic of intercession. In light of the pressing need for the gospel to go forth to the nations, Bertha and the committee knew their immediate action should be

58

She spent many hours on stage at conferences and ours one-on-one with people, but none of it happened without significant time on her knees talking to God. The hours she spent in prayer far outweighed those she spent on stage.[73] Bertha knew not everyone could go to the nations or give money towards sending missionaries, but everyone could pray. She knew prayer on behalf of the lost would be the driving force that would move hearts into action and move the world closer to Christ.

THE HOURS SHE SPENT IN PRAYER FAR OUTWEIGHED THOSE SHE SPENT ON STAGE.

In her passion to go, she fought fear, even in her own heart. In one of her speeches, she recalls a time in her life where she was not willing to give Jesus complete control. She had a terrible fear God would call her to do something she had no desire for. Eventually, Bertha gave Jesus full control of her future, whatever it held, and learned the peace of Jesus which stems from an obedient life.[74] She made plans to move abroad, yet when the Lord called her to stay and mobilize college students, she did.

Bertha's heart was to go, but she was willing to stay. She never used staying as an excuse to be complacent. Although she never went to the foreign mission field long- term, she worked to mobilize people all over the world for the work of Christ as either sacrificial goers or senders.

From December 31, 1919, to January 4, 1920, Bertha along with some of the world's leading mobilizers, John Mott, Robert Speer and Robert Wilder, spoke at the 8th International Convention of the Student Volunteer Movement for Foreign Missions (SVMFM). She gave a talk entitled *The Missionary Call.* In her presentation, Bertha states,

Although I have had the purpose all my life and directed all my thought and reading and study and definite planning toward getting out into a foreign field as a missionary, by the providence of God, I have never been allowed to go. I am thankful beyond any words that I had the purpose to go into the foreign field, because I think of

BERTHA'S HEART WAS TO GO, BUT SHE WAS WILLING TO STAY. SHE NEVER USED STAYING AS AN EXCUSE TO BE COMPLACENT.

girls all over this world who are out there, who would not have been out there if I had not had a chance to talk with them and to help them to go. And I am thankful that today I can say honestly that I am doing work in Turkey; that I am doing work in India; that I am doing work in China, through people who have been touched and impelled because God helped me years ago to form that purpose, to live the big life for foreign work.[75]

Bertha Conde never moved overseas as a permanent missionary, but she mobilized hundreds of men and women to go to the nations and share the gospel with the lost, thus reaching not one but multiple countries in her lifetime. In 1944 at the age of 73, Bertha Conde left this life to spend eternity with Jesus.

If ever there were words to sum up the life of Bertha Conde, it's these words she would challenge the audience with:

...... _F GIRLS ALL OVER THIS WORLD WHO ARE OUT THERE, WHO WOULD NOT HAVE BEEN OUT THERE IF I HAD NOT HAD A CHANCE TO TALK WITH THEM AND TO HELP THEM TO GO.

I may know what God's will is, if I am willing to come to Him in prayer. Now when I come to Him in prayer, I must not come with a set prayer upon my lips which I repeat before Him, wondering where the answer is. I must come into His presence with an attitude of mind of utter willingness to have Him speak to me, with His still small voice in my heart. I must come to Him willing to do the thing He shows me to do. I must come with a mind that is willing to go or willing to stay.[76]

Bertha was an ordinary woman who had a relationship with an extraordinary God. She was willing to go anywhere and do anything for Him. God used her life and time on this earth to make an eternal impact that is far greater than she could have ever imagined!

RUTH ROUSE

A Rally Call to Students
By Amber Joy & Natalie Crump

Whether we're 8, 18, or 88, no woman can deny how great it makes us feel to be invited to something we know will be memorable, fun and exciting. We love to be a part of things, especially things that matter and have implications of living our best life. Ruth Rouse gave this feeling of invitation to countless men and women throughout her lifetime. She mobilized others by inviting them into God's mission—and helping them see the value of their invitation.

As we reflect on women in missions history, Ruth Rouse is a hidden figure few have heard of. But even though her name might often be invisible in the credits of pioneer missions, her global impact is no less tangible than those of women like Amy Carmichael or Elisabeth Elliot. Ruth Rouse is described as "one who deserves an honorable place in this history [of missions]... missionary, evangelist, and pioneer in reaching students in countless universities and colleges around the world."[77] She was a woman whose willingness to simply say *yes* to God would leave thousands of university students around the world hungry to do the same.

Ruth Rouse was born in 1872 into an upper-middle-class family in London, England. She was one of five children born to George and Williamina Rouse. Even as a young child, her parents saw limitless potential in her. So when she showed interest in pursuing an education, they did all they could to empower her to go to school and become the natural-born pioneer they knew she would be. They sent her to schools with incredible reputations: First Notting Hill High School, Bedford College, and Girton College at the University of Cambridge. Little did she know how much God would leverage her university years in ways that would go far beyond simply being "well-educated."

Though her parents were deep people of faith, it wasn't until Ruth was eighteen years old that she committed her own life to Christ. After hearing the gospel presented by a layman at a

seaside service of the Children's Special Service Mission, she converted and was quickly baptized at the Metropolitan Tabernacle, where Charles H. Spurgeon preached every Sunday to thousands. After her baptism, she promptly joined the Church of England, where her parents were members.

While Ruth was at university, she was exposed to a mix of denominations, which affected the formation of her early Christian life. This varied involvement combined with exposure to God's global church set the stage for her future passion to see Christians unified worldwide.

63

In 1892, during her second year at Girton College, a man named Robert Wilder came to speak at Cambridge. Wilder was the son of missionaries and was on his way to India to spend his life as a missionary. "This gentle and modest young man of prayer had been instrumental in starting the rapidly growing Student Volunteer Movement (SVM)."[78] The SVM was an organization that desired to see the evangelization of the world during their generation. It focused on mobilizing college students to share the good news of the gospel where it had not been shared before.

Wilder spoke with passion and dedication to God's call to "make disciples of all nations" (Matthew 28:19). He challenged the students at Girton College to sign the SVM's pledge: "We are willing and desirous, God permitting, to become foreign missionaries." [79] Ruth's friend and schoolmate Agnes de Selincourt listened to Wilder's message and signed her declaration card right away. Ruth, however, was not as quick to sign. She understood the gravity of the call. If she pledged her life to God and was "willing and desirous to become a foreign missionary" as the SVM pledge stated, she knew she'd be forsaking everything for God.

She agonized over the decision and wrestled with fully surrendering her life to go where God led her, even if that meant to the ends of the earth. After two years of prayer and reflection, she signed the SVM pledge. After she signed,

> ...never again was there the slightest uncertainty in her mind that the purpose of God for her was worldwide and missionary, nor the faintest thought of changing her purpose to follow that will for her life.[80]

Even though she had grappled for two years with giving her *yes* to God, she was finally and completely willing to follow Him over oceans and into uncertain situations. Years later, when reflecting on this decisive moment, Ruth said that the Apostle Paul's words ran across her mind and heart: "I know whom I have believed, and am persuaded that He is able to keep that which I have committed unto Him against that day."[81] With God as her confidence and as her witness, Ruth knew she had made a commitment she would never break.

Ruth and her friend Agnes de Selincourt spent their remaining time at university as core members of the daily Girton College prayer meeting, fanning into flame their heart for God and His global purposes. She graduated in 1895 and immediately went to work for one year as an editor of *The Student Volunteer*, a British publication devoted to encouraging missions zeal among college students. After that year, she was invited to be a traveling speaker for the Student Volunteer Movement (SVM). It meant she would be away from home for many months, traveling from campus to campus and mobilizing thousands of college students to give their lives to missionary service. Even in light of the great cost such work would bring, Ruth of course said *yes.*

The leader of the SVM, John R. Mott, described the role of traveling speaker as one that required an "astonishing combination of qualities—administrative, promotive, scholastic, pastoral, teaching, inspirational, and prophetic."[82] Ruth embodied all of these traits, traveling extensively in 1897 to work with university students in Iceland, Denmark, Norway, Sweden, and Finland. Impressed by her impact among students, especially female students, Mott invited Ruth to come to the U.S. and Canada to continue mobilizing college students for another eighteen months.

Ruth exhorted students around the world to not just see the needs of their own country, but to look to the greater needs of those with no access to the gospel. She says,

> You are balancing home work against work in the foreign field. Remember that home claims have on their side all of the vividness of sight... Of the nature of foreign missionary work, on the other hand you can have but a vague notion — no words of appeal, written or spoken, have the force of need personally seen.[83]

She understood the needs of people who are far away can seem distant when compared to local needs, but she was passionate about communicating the deep need for the gospel where people had never heard of Jesus.

She dealt with these and other excuses from students head on. Her own family opposed her becoming a missionary; she knew other parents had similar concerns for their children, specifically their daughters. In response, Ruth states,

> I do not supposed there is a woman in the foreign field today, unless she may be a missionary's daughter, who has not had to face at one time, or another some kind of opposition from those that love her best; and just because they loved her best did they at first oppose this thing.[84]

SHE WAS NOT CALLING STUDENTS TO SOMETHING SHE WAS UNWILLING TO DO HERSELF, BUT EVEN MORE THAN BEING DEDICATED TO FOREIGN MISSIONS, RUTH WAS DEDICATED TO GOD.

Ruth was in the trenches with the students she ministered to. She was not calling them to something she was unwilling to do herself, but even more than being dedicated to foreign missions, Ruth was dedicated to God and passionate about following Him.

In 1899, Ruth signed up for foreign missionary service, putting her *yes* on the table and letting God put it on the map. She and her former classmate Agnes de Selincourt set sail for India and became pillar members of the Missionary Settlement for University Women at Bombay. Though her time as a missionary was limited to only two years due to poor health, Ruth worked tirelessly during the height of the bubonic plague to see Christian work started among the female students of South India.

As Ruth left India to regain her health in England, the next step for her life seemed far off. She had gone to the mission field as she'd pledged in college and had followed God to the "ends of the earth," but was unable to stay. What did God have in mind? How was she to serve the kingdom and the God's global mission from home? God provided the answer through John R. Mott and the Student Volunteer Movement.

Mott extended yet another invitation to Ruth: would she take a multi-country tour to study the conditions of women students, share the gospel with them, and recruit them to missions?[85] God had provided a clear path for her to continue her missionary service. With another *yes*, Ruth set out to go abroad.

This type of work marked the beginning of one of the most significant periods of her life. Her ability to not only preach the gospel and God's global vision to the masses, but also personally engage students, led her to another position as a leader in the World Student Christian Federation (WSCF), beginning in 1905. This was a position she would hold for 19 years as she ministered in over sixty-five countries. In 1906, she also became a member of the World Executive Committee for the YWCA, a post she remained in until 1946 and the last eight of those years serving as president.

While working for the SVM, WSCF, and YWCA, Ruth became one of the biggest proponents and organizers of student conferences. These conferences were a new tool in the hands of Christian workers who wanted to reach hundreds of students with the gospel and mobilize them to the Great Commission.

> Rouse observed that the conference "proved itself at once the most effective pioneering agency, the strongest evangelistic force, the best recruiting and training ground for leaders, and the focusing point of new ideas and fresh movements of the Spirit amongst students in generation after generation."[86]

For Ruth, the conferences were only successful if the students took the message and made an impact. She warned them to be men and women of the Word, to stand strong in the face of apathy and indifference, and pray. She says,

> We are going back to college, many of us, and are afraid that our lives will not bring froth 'fruit answerable to an amended life.' We shall have to prove the blessing we have received at the Conference; God will require it of us, and our fellow students will also require it... Dare we go forth without the weapon our Lord used? See that we answer our enemy as our Lord and Master answered him. "It is written, it is written." It is by constant, prayerful, persistent Bible study that our Lord will enable us to overcome.[87]

Ruth's deep commitment to organizing and speaking at conferences only made sense. While she was a university student, she herself had experienced God's work in her own life while attending conferences. In her opinion, the setting these conferences provided, where students from all walks of life gathered together, set the stage for God to do amazing things. She recalls,

> Some students were willing, eager for light, seeking God and His way for them. Some were dragged by friends sorely against their own inclination, but they too found a way... That's where God found me. That's when I found my life's work.[88]

Throughout all of her ministry work, Ruth sought gender equality. She truly believed in the power of women. Ruth was part of a generation of women who, for the first time, saw a glimpse of what equality between men and women could look like. "She saw the unique opportunities of her time and acted upon them."[89] Living outside the bounds of cultural standards, as she was a single woman in missionary work, she consistently called for "mixed leadership of men and women in all student groups" and "spoke of the day when men and women would be considered equal human beings working side by side for the cause of Christ."[90]

In her role with the YWCA, Ruth championed the value of women reaching other women. She empowered its members with a spirit of independence to take the gospel to the ends of the earth. Her own singleness gave her authority to speak into other young women's lives who thought they had to choose between marriage or missions. She set an example for younger girls, proving that they did not have to conform to societal norms, but instead could be used by God while married or single to reach the world. Ruth's own track record of following God, no matter the cost, gave them the courage to do the same.

After spending much of the final years of her life as an historian, documenting the history of the student volunteers, Ruth Rouse passed away in 1950. She was one of the most respected women in her field and is often compared to John R. Mott, who not only was her trusted co-laborer and the leader of the largest missions movement in history, but who also went on to win the Nobel Peace Prize for his work among university students around the world.

RUTH'S OWN TRACK RECORD OF FOLLOWING GOD, NO MATTER THE COST, GAVE THEM THE COURAGE TO DO THE SAME.

Though she might not have received the same recognition as Mott, Ruth arguably had similar influence. Those around her would say her life was radical, but she would say it was merely humble obedience. Nevertheless, it cannot be denied that hers was a life that showed how powerfully God could move through just one person who was willing to say *yes*.

Listen to Ruth's plea to a group of female students at a conference in 1901. She exhorts them to put their own *yes* on the table:

> If you are a Christian woman, you have absolutely no right to hold that life as your own. It is not yours any more than the dress that belongs to a friend is yours; and if you are holding is as your own possession, you are holding it not by right, but by robbery... Oh, I ask every woman in the room today to fill out that other sentence, "I so love that I give"—what? A little time, a little

strength, a little money, or my life? Your gift will be the measure of your love.[91]

What is your measure of love, of devotion, of sacrifice you're willing to give to God? Would you be so bold, like Ruth, to put your own yes on the table and let God put it on the map?

GRACE WILDER

The Hidden Secret to a Movement

By Ivy Amanda

Do you ever feel unnoticed? Unless something you do is visible or goes viral, do you wonder how much it really mattered? This story of Grace Wilder confronts the self-promotion we see and struggle with so much today. She is an example of a woman whose hidden obedience brought about lasting, powerful, and public impact.

The Student Volunteer Movement (SVM) was perhaps history's greatest mobilization movement. 100,000 college students were raised up to give themselves to the evangelization of the world in their generation. During the life of this movement, one out of every thirty-five college students were recruited to the foreign field. According to its leader, John R. Mott, the success of the movement should be attributed to one person, Grace Wilder.[92] Here is her story.

In 1886 there arose in the hearts of a few Christian leaders the desire to see Christian college students harnessed into a force, discipled in godliness, and mobilized to the nations. A man named Luther Wishard was the initiator of that vision. His plan was to host a summer training project. D.L. Moody would be the keynote speaker. 251 individually-selected college students from 89 colleges attended. The students, as a rule, were to be men in their freshman or sophomore year. One exception was made in order to have the attendance of Robert Wilder, a senior at Princeton and known missions zealot.

During the conference, held in Mount Hermon, Massachusetts, the Holy Spirit began to move on the young men's hearts and soon there was a large group of students committing themselves to a career in missions. Wilder kept track of their numbers by writing this declaration on individual cards and having them sign it. The declaration stated, "We, the undersigned, declare ourselves willing and desirous, God permitting, to go to the unevangelized portions of the world."[93] On the final day of the conference, Robert Wilder, along

WE, THE UNDERSIGNED, DECLARE OURSELVES WILLING AND DESIROUS, GOD PERMITTING, TO GO TO THE UNEVANGELIZED PORTIONS OF THE WORLD.

with each man who'd signed his declaration, held a prayer of consecration. Wilder counted them. The group had grown to one hundred men devoted to world evangelization. They came to be known as the Mount Herman 100. The decision was made to try and sustain this move of God by sending delegates back to the campuses to influence other students with a vision for the nations. Robert Wilder was chosen, along with a few other men, and this marked the beginning of the Student Volunteer Movement.

 The story not often heard, however, is of Robert's sister, Grace Wilder. She was one of those most precious of the Lord's gems whose only contentment was to be hidden that He might receive the praise.

Grace's parents, Royal and Eliza Wilder, sailed to India as missionaries in 1846. After years of service they continued to delay leaving India to return home, despite the impending threat of an Indian revolt. Only when Royal came down with cholera did he consent return to America. The war broke out the very next day. The life of Grace Wilder was spared as she was born in 1861, shortly after their arrival in Saratoga Springs, New York.

Grace grew up in an environment where missionary zeal was instilled as part of the normal Christian life. She attended Mt. Holyoke College, an institute for women which was known for its influencing and training young women for the mission field. It has been said by a former student that Mt. Holyoke was a "missionary factory!" It is true. In its beginning years from 1837 to 1887, 178 graduates served in the foreign fields. Grace was one of those. She played a pivotal part in encouraging and training the young women to go. In fact, Grace held a Bible study on campus and the girls' watch-cry was, "We hold ourselves willing and desirous to go wherever the Lord may call us, even if it be in the foreign land."[94] Grace was also a member of the Mount Holyoke Missionary Association (MHMA), a group for women who were interested in missions, which met in secret, "because of reticence about

74

letting people know that they were considering foreign missionary service."[95] In 1898, women from the MHMA had been sent to "South Africa, East Africa, China, Turkey, and India."[96]

One of her greatest investments of spiritual energy was in her younger brother, Robert. Her strong conviction about the urgent call of Christ to make disciples among all nations proved time again to be a stronghold for Robert. During Robert's college years at Princeton, his desire was to awaken in his fellow classmates a spiritual revival and, more specifically, a missions movement. This led Robert to start a missionary organization that met at his parents' home. Faithfully and humbly in the secret of the next room, Grace labored to bring the men before the Lord in prayer. It was these meetings that would later provide the structure for the Student Volunteer Movement.

Robert was a senior when he received his invitation to attend the conference at Mt. Hermon. By this time, his father was very ill and burdened with the job of publishing a monthly missions magazine known as *The Missionary Review*. Without Robert's assistance at home, the *Review* and his father's health were sure to suffer. It was an incredibly pressing need that almost kept Robert from attending the conference. Were it not for the urging of his sister who saw clearly Mt. Hermon might be God's answer to their prayers, Robert may have missed his opportunity.

John Mott says of this time,

> She discerned that conditions were going to be furnished at Mount Hermon that might make possible the generation of a great movement, and she laid upon her brother and upon some of the other Princeton men who were to attend the

conference, the burden of prayer and expectati
and charged them before God to persevere in prayer
and effort that this Mount Hermon gathering might
not close without the inauguration of a missionary
movement that in some sense would be worthy of
the wonderful situation then confronting the
Church on the foreign field.[97]

While Robert was away, Grace stepped in to write *The
Missionary Review* and care for her ailing father. It is
recorded the year prior to the conference Robert and Grace
met nightly to pray for a stirring of missionary conviction
across the campuses of the United States. Her specific
prayer during the conference was that the small core of
committed men would grow in number to 100—the exact
number that were recruited.[98]

In the closing remarks of her pastor on the occasion of
Grace's death, he states,

> I am privileged to mention what is known to but
> very few, namely, Miss Wilder's relation to the
> Student Volunteer Movement. This movement
> started in connection with the Northfield Student
> Movement. In the years 1884-86 she and her
> brother, Robert, while at Princeton spent many a
> night in prayer to God for a great missionary
> awakening in the colleges, and asked God for
> volunteers for the mission field. At the Mt. Hermon
> Conference in 1886 one hundred students signed
> the volunteer pledge and out of this beginning grew
> a movement, which today is so widely affecting the
> whole missionary enterprise. Others are receiving
> the praise for this movement. We should not forget
> that God redeemed His promise of answering
> prayer, and this was the faithful and effectual

prayer of Miss Wilder and her brother, which, humanly speaking, began this work.[99]

In the year following the conference, it was presented to Robert that he might be the a traveling speaker to college campuses. He would challenge those men and women who did not attend, as well as encourage the volunteers who signed the declaration cards. Now, facing the demands of an extremely strenuous year of constant travel, he had to consider his own grueling battle of several years with poor health. Also, his year-long absence would most likely mean he would never see his father again; the doctors were giving his father six months. Grace was one of his few faithful supporters in his conviction to undertake this work, and their correspondence through the next year proved an incredible encouragement to him.

Not long after this climax of events did Grace sail for the foreign field herself. In 1887, at twenty-six, Grace and her widowed mother set off for Islampur, India. That year she wrote, *Shall I Go? Thoughts for Girls*, for the Student Volunteer Movement's literature series. [100] In it she dismantles the top excuses hindering women from missions.

Many of the issues she addressed are still barriers for women today. She challenged women, stating,

> But just what is our great work as women of this nineteenth century? Our Savior has died and risen. The door of heaven is open to every poor sinner. "Whosoever shall call upon the name of the Lord shall be saved." Yet millions of women know not this wonderful truth. And why not? Christian women have not told them.[101]

She addressed issues such as what is the missionary call, the fear of being unqualified, and a desire to stay home. She urged women to overcome these barriers with the truth of scripture, appeals to logic, statistics about the state of the unevangelized world, and compassion for the lost.

While addressing the fear of not being qualified, she wrote,

> 1 Cor. 1:18-31 mentions five things which God uses: The weak, foolish, base, and despised things, and things that are not... Our only fear need be that we are not offering to God the very best we have.[102]

Grace also addressed the barrier of Christian parents not wanting their children to move overseas. To this she simply asked,

> Christian mothers, will you not give us up in such a crisis? Instead of sending us to a studio or a conservatory will you not support us in harems and zenanas, that we may gather jewels, even King's daughters, from the ends of the earth?[103]

Grace was unwilling to allow these barriers to keep others from joining her in taking action to finish the Great Commission in their lifetime.

Throughout her life, Grace continued to mobilize others to join her overseas. At a Student Volunteer Movement conference in 1896, she addressed the need for more workers to come to India. She provided current statistics and challenged the attendees with the need for longtime workers in India. Grace declared, "It is not enough for missionaries to make an occasional village tour. We need workers who will live in a simple way for the people, among the people."[104]

As Grace worked with Indians who had little to no access to Christian teaching, she was face-to-face with the reality that the harvest was plentiful, but the laborers were few. Her response? Mobilize more missionaries. To this she gave her life.

IT IS NOT ENOUGH FOR MISSIONARIES TO MAKE AN OCCASIONAL VILLAGE TOUR. WE NEED WORKERS WHO WILL LIVE IN A SIMPLE WAY FOR THE PEOPLE, AMONG THE PEOPLE.

Grace died in India in 1911 at the age of fifty. She stands as an example of the quiet confidence that comes in knowing and being aligned with the will of God. Her short life, though known by few, reflects the image of One who, hidden and meek came to seek and to save the lost. John Mott said,

I have seen so many unknown, humble missionaries working in quiet places who have held their lives in such close relationship to God that He has been able by His Holy Spirit to break through these lives and extend His influence in a way far beyond our comprehension.[105]

Miss Grace Wilder was one such as these.

Her absolute surrender to and joy in her Father's work are summed up in this small poem she herself wrote called *The Secret of God's Will.*

THE SECRET OF GOD'S WILL

I sought the secret of Thy will;
But, Lord, I did not know
Thy lowly life—Thy heavy cross—
Life's plan and purpose show.

I thought some special path and plan,
Bearing my name I'd see;
Instead I found in Jesus' life
Footprints for such as me.

To save the lost His aim, so mine,
Poor, hungry ones to feed;
Weak, sightless eyes to turn to light;
Sore, erring feet to lead.

Since Jesus' life reveals God's will,
Surely I'm in His way,
When choosing rough, dark mountain paths
To find the sheep who stray.

To be like Him, I ask to hold
My light where it is dark,
To carry bread to those passed by;
Let this, Lord, be my part.

Thus preaching Christ where yet unknown,
God's worldwide love I show;
And since for this Christ lived and died,
God's will for me I know.

ESTHER AHN KIM

Weak Made Strong
By Natalie Francis

Have you ever considered why you were born when you were, where you were, or to whom? Our time and place is not coincidental. Our next woman's was not either, and neither was her name. Much of her story mirrors the biblical story of Esther who, facing her fear of death, realized God had her here "for such a time as this," Her perspective was, "If I perish, I perish."

Esther Ahn Kim had the privilege of suffering for her faith under the occupation of Korea by the Japanese in the early 20th century. While many Christians feared suffering, Esther moved toward it. She never wavered at the possibility of dying for the gospel. Through fear, persecution, and torture, Esther is an example of a joy-filled life fully surrendered to the will of God.

Esther, known in her native Korean name as Ahn Ei Sook, was born June 24, 1908, into a wealthy family in modern-day North Korea. Her family's wealth and influence enabled Esther to

82

attend an elite girls' school in Korea, as well as higher education in Japan. Esther gained confidence in the Japanese language and culture and established relationships with influential people through her family connections. Her father was not a Christian, but her mother was a strong follower of Jesus. After her studies in Japan, Esther became a teacher at a Christian school back in Korea.

Between 1876 and 1910, through a series of treaties and other policies, Japan slowly took control of Korea. Japan also decreed specific cultural and religious policies that marginalized the Korean language and culture. On August 22, 1910, Japan

officially made Korea part of their empire. In 1939, as World War II took over the world stage, the security of Christians in Korea was at risk. Japan imposed an order in Korea demanding everyone to worship the Japanese "sun-god." Disobedience to this decree meant death.

Meanwhile, Esther was teaching at a school for girls in the city of Pyongyang, Korea when the entire school was ordered to walk to a shrine and worship the "sun-god." Esther's life, as well as the lives of the other Christian students and teachers were at risk. She faced a life-altering decision—to give in to the pressures of the Japanese and worship their god, or lay down everything for her faith regardless of the consequences. The local police waited and watched to ensure they obeyed the order to worship. Esther stood while others bowed. While standing she said to God, "Today on the mountain, before the large crowd, I will proclaim there is no other god but You."[106] Esther counted the cost and knew her decision would result in imprisonment or death.

As soon as Esther returned to the school. She was arrested. They brought her to the district chief. During the interrogation, the district chief got a phone call. While he was on the phone, Esther felt led to do something daring. She stood and began to walk out of the office. To her astonishment, no one stopped her. She kept walking! In that moment she realized God would indeed guide her.

Esther fled and hid in the countryside. During this season, she fought fear of arrest and torture. She struggled to remain steadfast in her faith. She speaks of her perspective during this period:

> I began to think that life might be worth living in this time of persecution. It might even be a truer picture of the believer to agonize, to suffer, to be hated and tortured, and even to be killed in obeying God's words rather that to live an ordinary, uneventful life. [107]

Esther continued to count the cost of following Jesus and always found Him worthy.

For a time, Esther was safe in the countryside. She memorized songs and scripture, and met with other Christians in secret. However, persecution continued to escalate. She heard stories of Christians being tortured for their faith. In light of her public stand against the Japanese sun-god and her disregard of Japanese rule, she knew her capture was imminent. She began to fast and pray. She asked God to work through her in His power. To help her stand strong in her faith. With each fast, Esther's resolve to die for her faith became stronger.

The Japanese authorities discovered her location. She had to flee. As she journeyed, she heard God say "Go to Pyongyang."

Esther knew returning to Pyongyang would be dangerous. The Japanese presence was strong in the region; yet Esther obeyed.

When she arrived in the Pyongyang train station, she saw a large group of Japanese soldiers. She was sure they would recognize her and arrest her. To her surprise, they did not notice her. She was struck by their faces. They were young men who served a corrupt empire bent on destroying God's people. She thought, "Who will tell these men that they are on a path of destruction against God?"[108]

Esther felt burdened to warn the Japanese leaders of their idolatry. She said during this time,

> the Bible said that the wages of [sin and] idolatry were wars, famines, and pestilences... Because of it, youth would die in wars, young wives would become widows, parents would lose their sons, children would become orphans, and peace would vanish. Idolatry would cause all the world to be visited with calamities.[109]

The task was too great for just her. She needed help. God answered her by bringing alongside a friend and helper, Elder Park. He encouraged her and mentored her,

> God wants to warn the Japanese. You are an excellent speaker in their language... I want to walk before you... and show you what faith is and how a believer should die for his God.[110]

Esther once again was validated in her calling. She knew her imprisonment was near and she began to prepare. She chose to hope in the promises of God instead of the empty security of this life.

In Pyongyang, she had the privilege of being reunited with her mother! Her mother did not hesitate to encourage her. She said,

> Concerning your going to warn the Japanese authorities, I can think of many things that make me feel that God has planned this for you since you were a child.[111]

As persecution of Christians intensified, Esther's mother confirmed, "The time has come for you to prepare yourself to die." [112] She encouraged Esther leave Korea and go to Japan to share the gospel, even in the face of imprisonment, persecution, and death.

Soon after both Esther and Elder Park set out for Japan. They were under police watch, but made it all the way to Japan without arrest. Elder said to Esther,

> Don't you see it yet?... The Lord is my refuge. God has blinded all the Japanese people in order to hide me from them. What can blind people see?[113]

IT MIGHT EVEN BE A TRUER PICTURE OF THE BELIEVER TO AGONIZE, TO SUFFER, TO BE HATED AND TORTURED, AND EVEN TO BE KILLED IN OBEYING GOD'S WORDS RATHER THAT TO LIVE AN ORDINARY, UNEVENTFUL LIFE.

Elder's faith in God challenged Esther. Believers she knew in Korea were aware death could come to them as Christians suffered persecution, but Elder seemed to be running toward death in an effort to make Jesus Christ known to the Japanese.

Upon arrival in Japan, Esther and Elder found favor with key leaders willing to listen. They met with the Lieutenant General of the Salvation Army, the Deputy General of Korea, and congressmen. One General, General Hibiki, was so moved by

Esther and Elder's account of persecution and oppression the Koreans experienced as a result of Japanese rule, he arranged a time for them to speak at an upcoming event with all the political leaders from the Japanese empire. Grievously, Esther and Elder missed their allotted time.

This, however, would not stop them. The Japanese officials had to be warned. They decided to walk right in and began to speak. Stunned, the political leaders agreed. Esther and Elder shared three points. First, the Japanese government should repent and withdraw its harsh rulership from Korea. Second, they needed to examine which is the true religion—Shintoism or Christianity. The third was a radical idea to grab their attention. They suggested burning a stack of wood and throw a Shinto believer and Esther on it. The one who is not burned shall prove the true religion. To no one's surprise, they were both arrested immediately.

After several weeks, they were sent back to Korea and put in Japanese-controlled prisons. Esther's mother visited her and told her about the harsh oppression and torture prisoners at Pyongyang were experiencing. Immediately, Esther demanded to be transferred there. On September 20, 1940, her request was granted, and Esther was transferred to the famously foul prison in Pyongyang.

The smell alone took a week to adjust to; their meals were a mixture of grains and sand. Prisoners lived in tight quarters that would freeze during the winter and swelter in the summer. Torture was daily and normal. Then a sickness called the Manchurian flu spread throughout Korea. The flu seemed to target the prison guards in charge of torturing. This happened so frequently no guards would torture the prisoners because they were afraid they would catch the flu and die. The oppression Esther faced only strengthened her. She stated:

I now realized that the more dangerous my situation became, the closer God would be to me. The harsher my torture, the more the Lord would comfort me. Up to this moment I had believe in the Lord with all my heart. Now the time had come for me to experience the work of faith. I was now to see the promises of the Lord become mine. He would care for me.[114]

Esther was a shepherd to her fellow prisoners. Each of these relationships was built by fasting, prayer, and sacrifice. She shared about Jesus and taught them to rely on God. Christians were strengthened in their faith in Jesus and unified by their trust in His power. It was clear God was going before and behind Esther's actions to protect her and ultimately to bring Himself glory.

A young women named Wha Choon was imprisoned for murdering her husband. Esther requested she be transferred to her cell. Wha Choon seemed insane and inconsolable, but Esther showed her the compassion of Christ. She gave her food rations to Choon and held her when she raged and screamed. Choon was set free of evil spirits and gave her life to Jesus before she was executed. God moved mightily in the prison in Pyongyang.

One prison guard, Kane, was so impacted by the peace she saw that she gave her life to Jesus. Kane realized the Christians inside the prison were more peaceful than anyone she knew outside the prison. Esther said, "The Lord had changed a dreadful jailer [Kane], making her my closest protector."[115] Esther continued to be tortured until her release.

After six years of imprisonment, Esther was set free. On April 15, 1945, Japan signed an unconditional surrender. With this surrender, the Christians were freed. As the prisoners left Pyongyang, a guard announced,

Ladies and gentlemen! These are the ones who for six long years refused to worship Japanese gods. They fought against severe torture, hunger, and cold, and have won out without bowing their heads to the idol worship of Japan. Today they are champions of faith.[116]

The waiting crowd shouted, "Praise the name of Jesus!" and sang together:

All hail the power of Jesus' name!
Let angels prostrate fall.
Bring forth the royal diadem
And crown him Lord of all.[117]

As Japan withdrew from Korea at the end of World War II, Russia became a problem. Russian communists installed a brutal regime with the North while the Americans controlled the South. The dividing line between North and South Korea is called the 38th parallel. Large numbers of Koreans from the North sought refuge below the 38th parallel line. Koreans in the north chose to abandon their property and flee south rather than remain in Communist North. During the transition of power, Russian communists kidnapped Esther because she was a well-known Christian leader. Esther, however, escaped and fled back to South Korea. South Korea became a refuge to many Christians, including Esther and her family.

Soon, Esther was offered multiple employment propositions in ministry. She turned them all down until one day an American, Phyllis Coe, convinced her to leave South Korea to share her story with churches across the United States. Esther agreed. Her fame increased especially after a pamphlet she wrote called *If I Perish*. The pamphlet told her story. This resource spread from the United States to Canada, England, Australia, and

South America. During this time, Esther met and married an engineer named Kim Don Mung. He would later become a pastor and help found the Brenda Street Baptist Church in Los Angeles.

Throughout her life, Esther was given countless opportunities from God to say "*yes*" to His will over her own. Esther said *yes* to God as she refused to bow down to the Japanese sun-god. Esther said *yes* to God when she went to Japan to warn the leaders of their sin. Esther said *yes* to God by asking to be transferred to the more severe prison in Pyongyang. She said *yes* to God when she was tortured for her faith instead of worshipping the emperor. She said *yes* to God by giving up her food for other prisoners so they would know the kindness of God. Esther could have decided then that she had done enough for God—that she had sacrificed enough—but she continued to use her life as a vessel for Him and to make Him known. Esther gave her life to God even in the fearful moments. In the moments she wanted to give up and walk away, she pushed harder into God and relied on His strength. She knew in her own strength she was weak, but in God, His power is made perfect in our weakness (2 Corinthians 12:9).

IN THE MOMENTS SHE WANTED TO GIVE UP AND WALK AWAY, SHE PUSHED HARDER INTO GOD AND RELIED ON HIS STRENGTH.

Esther exemplifies a life of complete abandonment; a life wholly surrendered to the Kingdom of Heaven coming to earth. Let us take Esther's life as an example and prepare to die daily to ourselves for the sake of the gospel.

DARLENE DEIBLER ROSE

Embracing the Mystery of God's Plan

By Abbie Brock

To this point in your life, how long is your list already of the "Why" questions you have for God? How many of us feel that if we only knew His reasons behind the hard things in our lives, we could make it? In her book Evidence Not Seen, *Darlene Deibler Rose speaks to countless instances in her life where things happening around her didn't make sense, but how she chose to persevere and trust sets her apart as a remarkable example of walking with God by faith and not by sight.*

Darlene was only ten years old, but her heart was burning as the speaker challenged the high school students to give their lives to God for missionary service. Why couldn't she be older? If she were, she would gladly go!

Only the year before, she and her mother heard the same speaker, Dr. R. R. Brown, speaking on the radio about Christ.

92

That broadcast led them to a local church, which in turn led them to God.

Now, as she sat and listened at the missionary convention, she felt a hand on her shoulder. She turned to find no one, and immediately knew it was the Lord. Darlene quietly asked Him, "What is it, Lord?" The response came, "My child, would you go anywhere for Me, no matter what it cost?" Without hesitation and with great awe and wonder, she replied, "Lord, I'd go anywhere for You, no matter what it cost!"[118] Not many years later, Darlene learned the cost of following Jesus, first in missionary service, and then as a prisoner of the Japanese in World War II. Her faith, though challenged and tested, never wavered and became the "evidence of things not seen" (Hebrews 11:1) for all who observed her life.

By age nineteen, Darlene was in school for missionary service

and was determined she would never marry. That is, until she met Russell Deibler, a missionary to Borneo, an island in East Asia. After their first date, Darlene was convinced he was the man for her, and they were married soon after.

After six months of language and culture training, Russell and Darlene sailed for the Netherlands East Indies, current-day Indonesia and Papua New Guinea. They arrived in Java on their one-year anniversary. Darlene was twenty-one. Russell and fellow missionary Walter Post began expeditions into the jungle to prepare for the work. The trek was arduous, grueling, and dangerous. When Russell and Walter returned a couple months later, Russell had lost sixty pounds and had developed an infection on the bottom of his feet. It was diagnosed as Jungle Rot. In order for his feet to heal, each day Darlene had to painfully tear off all the layers of dead tissue to get to the raw flesh underneath. She was reminded of the scripture, "How beautiful upon the mountains are the feet of him who brings good news" (Isaiah 52:7). She longed for the day when she could accompany her husband to the interior of the jungle.

As the men continued to explore the interior of the jungle God led them to a tribe known as the Kapaukaus. Darlene soon was able to join them in the work. She was the first woman to ever venture this far in. Greeted with roasted sweet potatoes, Darlene felt she had at last come home. She and Russell loved living with the Kapaukus and sharing the good news with them. They worked hard to master the language as quickly as possible. A little building was erected that served as a schoolhouse and church building. Sunday services were well attended. They were also able to meet other villagers living along the rivers.

They kept up with current events by tuning into the radio. On May 10, 1940, Darlene's twenty-third birthday, they heard the news the Nazis were invading Holland. Five days later, Holland fell, and they knew their time with the Kapaukus would be cut short. All too soon, word came they had to leave the village. With heavy hearts they packed their few belongings and headed out of the jungle to Macassar. Darlene was comforted during this time by Jeremiah 29:11, "I know the thoughts that I think toward you... thoughts of peace and not of evil." It would be ten years before she would return.

Russell was voted into a leadership position within the mission organization, which would require them to stay in Macassar. Neither Russell nor Darlene wanted the position, desiring instead to return to the jungle as soon as possible. However, Darlene was reminded of her commitment to go anywhere for the Lord. She said,

> My longing to return... I surrendered to the Lord,
> put it in my *Mystery Box*, and closed the lid. I
> would be remaining in Macassar by His
> appointment and I could trust the future to Him.[119]

This was just one of many mysteries she would entrust to the Lord over the next few years.

As the war got closer and closer to home, the missionaries decided to move further inland, away from the vulnerable coast. In early 1942, they still had high hopes the conflict would be short. They only took enough supplies to last them a few months. When given an opportunity to evacuate by the Dutch police, Russell, Darlene, and their band of missionaries prayed individually about whether to stay or to leave. When the truck came to take them to the ship, not one of them went. A few days later they heard the evacuation ship had been torpedoed and sunk, leaving no survivors! They realized why God had directed them to stay. Darlene wrote,

> It is imperative that we know the voice of the
> Shepherd and learn to follow Him when He speaks.
> We must be obedient, not matter what He says to
> us: it may even mean our life.[120]

IT IS IMPERATIVE THAT WE KNOW THE VOICE OF THE SHEPHERD AND LEARN TO FOLLOW HIM WHEN HE SPEAKS.

Soon after the Japanese invasion was complete, soldiers arrived and declared them prisoners. They could not leave their residence, nor could they have any contact with anyone outside the premises. Some time later, they transferred the men into the back of a truck to be taken to another camp. Dr. Jaffray alone remained of the male missionaries, as he was believed to be too old and too sick to matter. Darlene was able

95

to grab a few things for Russell before he left. Russell's parting words to Darlene were, "Remember one thing, dear: God said that He would never leave us nor forsake us."[121] She would never see Russell again.

The two had already been separated so much and for Russell to be taken so abruptly from her, the hurt was beyond imagination. As she struggled to believe all things work together for good, she sought refuge in the Lord's presence. In that moment, God reminded her of her promise as a child to go anywhere with Him, no matter the cost. How naïve she had been when she had made that promise! Yet, she knew her commitment remained the same even with her greater understanding of the cost. She determined to leave the cost up to her Father, and in that moment He took the sting and bitterness away. Another mystery locked away in her *Mystery Box* for the Lord's safe keeping.

For the rest of 1942, the women and Dr. Jaffray lived on the conference grounds, growing food to avoid starvation, fighting off rats and local bandits, and surviving the harassment of Japanese officers. Over and over again they saw God perform little miracles that reminded them He indeed never does leave nor forsake His children.

In early 1943, they were moved to Kampili, a former tuberculosis sanitarium. Darlene was assigned to Barracks 8 with anyone else who was not Dutch and was appointed barracks leader. Although she was only twenty-five at the time, she quickly earned the respect and appreciation of many. On the first night, Darlene established the practice of daily Bible reading and prayer to close the day. This devotional time set the tone for their community and fostered a spirit of compassion and unity within Barracks.[122]

In Kampili, every prisoner had a job. Darlene describes what it was like:

> A certain number of women had to be assigned to working in the central kitchen, hospital kitchen, and camp gardens; and to clearing the land, felling trees, working on the roads, unloading the trucks, raising pigs and chickens, pumping water, sewing knitting, cooking porridge, boiling water, doing hospital duties and nursing.[123]

Each barracks had a quota, and Darlene worked out a system, assigning each woman different jobs each day based on how healthy they were. Illness, starvation, poor mental and emotional health, were just a few of the things threatening their survival.

Mr. Yamaji was the Japanese officer assigned as Commander of Kampili. His reputation preceded him as a man who would not hesitate to kill prisoners. Darlene and the others learned firsthand about his irate temper. The entire camp was assembled and forced to watch as Mr. Yamaji beat a man to death. The women were finally dismissed, demoralized, sickened, and with a healthy respect of Mr. Yamaji's anger.

Because of her leadership role, Darlene had significant interaction with Mr. Yamaji. She slowly gained his respect. In late 1943, Darlene received news her husband had died. Mr. Yamaji observed even in death Darlene had hope. She shared the gospel with him, even suggesting she had been brought to Kampili specifically to tell him about Jesus. Mr. Yamaji, moved to tears, quickly left the room. Darlene knew from then on Mr. Yamaji was her friend. Years later, after the war, Darlene heard about a transformed Mr. Yamaji who was sharing the gospel on Japanese radio! Even in the midst of great sorrow for Darlene, God was working. She knew He never wastes pain and suffering.

In the spring of 1944, a shiny black limousine pulled up to Kampili and dread fell over the camp. Two military police officers, members of the feared Kenpeitai, the most brutal group of the Japanese army, stepped out and disappeared into the camp office. A few weeks before they had come and whisked away two of Darlene's fellow missionaries, Margaret and Philoma. This time, the limousine had come for Darlene. They thought she was a spy. They transported her to the horrific Kenpeitai prison and locked her in a cell on death row. Suffering from dysentery, and malaria, she endured months of torture and interrogations.

Darlene never broke down in front of the soldiers. Once she returned to her cell, she cried and poured out her heart before the Lord. Her Bible had been taken from her, so she only had what she committed to memory. After each interrogation, she thought there was no way she could survive another. Each time, the Lord gently reminded her, "My child, My grace is sufficient for thee. Not *was*, nor *shall be*, but it *is* sufficient."[124]

When she was desperate for fresh air, she would climb up and look out the window above the door. One day, she watched someone smuggle a bunch of bananas through the vine-covered fence. Darlene's daily diet consisted only of a cup of worm-infested rice porridge. When she saw those bananas, she instantly began to crave them and prayed she could have just one banana. Almost immediately, she began thinking of all the reasons God wouldn't be able to provide a banana. She took back what she thought was a foolish prayer. The very next day her cell was unlocked and opened to reveal Mr. Yamaji from Kampili! Her appearance had been so altered that Mr. Yamaji's eyes filled with tears. Just seeing his smiling, friendly face was like warm sunshine to Darlene. After he left, to her great surprise and joy, bananas were brought and laid at her feet. Not just one banana or even one bunch of bananas, but ninety-two bananas! A gift from Mr. Yamaji. Darlene was overcome with her lack of trust in God's omnipotence and was reminded that He delights to do "exceedingly abundantly above all we ask or think" (Ephesians 3:20).

Darlene's prison cell was transformed into a sanctuary where she experienced God's presence in every troubled hour. One day, she sat praising and thanking God for His sustaining presence. She suddenly felt an emptiness. Where was God? Why couldn't she feel His calm comforting presence? She began searching her heart, worried there was some hidden sin she had not confessed. 1 John 3:21 was brought to her mind, "Beloved, if our heart does not condemn us, we have confidence before God." She then remembered Numbers 23:19,

> God is not man, that He should lie, or a son of man, that He should change His mind. Has He said, and will He not do it? Or has He spoken, and will He not fulfill it?

I DO NOT NEED TO *FEEL* YOU NEAR, BECAUSE YOUR WORD SAYS YOU WILL NEVER LEAVE ME NOR FORSAKE ME. LORD, I CONFIRM MY FAITH; I BELIEVE.

Darlene prayed,

Lord, I believe all that the Bible says. I do walk by faith and not by sight. I do not need to *feel* You near, because Your word says You will never leave me nor forsake me. Lord, I confirm my faith; I believe.[125]

Again, scripture came to mind, "Now faith is the substance of things hoped for, the evidence of things not seen" (Hebrews 11:1). God was teaching her a valuable lesson. Darlene's hope was not in things seen, not in feelings or emotions, but in evidence *not* seen, in the Person of Jesus Christ!

At this time the Lord gave her 2 Corinthians 1:10: "Who delivered... and does deliver... He will yet deliver." Slowly she realized God meant to deliver her from the hands of the Kenpeitai! Then a guard came and told her she was being taken somewhere else. They gathered Margaret and Philoma, as well, and took them to the secret police headquarters. They were fed a "last meal" and forced to write a confession of their crimes, at the dictation of the Japanese. Darlene was lined up against a wall while charges were read against her. She was sentenced to death. As the officer began to draw his sword to execute her, a car suddenly pulled up in front of the headquarters and chaos ensued. Suddenly, Darlene was marched out of the building and into a waiting car, along with Margaret and Philoma, and they were on their way back to Kampili prison. The Lord had delivered them, just as He had revealed He would! She never found out what had happened and why her life had been spared. Another mystery for her *Mystery Box*.

Back in Kampili, Darlene's health was near death. She weighed a mere sixty pounds. She was committed to meet her work quota and even continued as barracks leader. Despite her health, life in Kampili returned to some manner of normalcy.

As the war stretched into 1945, air raids became more and more frequent. They spent more and more time in trenches. Everyone began to wonder if the war was nearing the end. They had no access to what was happening in the outside world. They could only speculate. As the air raids increased, they continued to fight for survival. Finally, in September 1945, Mr. Yamaji assembled them all and announced the war was over. Japan had accepted the terms for surrender. There were no wild and jubilant celebrations like there were in the United States.

Instead, silent tears were shed, and the women embraced each other in quiet disbelief and gratefulness.

The evacuation of the prisoners began shortly after. Darlene was able to stay long enough to visit Russell's grave and meet some of the men he had befriended. She heard story after story of how Russell ministered to the men around him, even while in prison. Darlene and Russell were only married six years, separated for three of those. By visiting his grave and meeting the men who remember him, Darlene felt that she had been given a very sweet gift. Indeed she had.

Darlene arrived back in the U.S. in November of 1945, where she was welcomed eagerly by her parents. At the age of twenty-eight she was widowed, emaciated, emotionally fatigued, and without a single material possession. The cost had been great. Darlene began to speak and testify of how God's presence and power had sustained her as a prisoner.

During her evacuation from Indonesia, she felt convinced she would return. Her days of missionary service were not yet over. She wasn't in the U.S. very long before God brought another man into her life, Gerald Rose, who also wanted to serve as a missionary in the region she was in. They were married in 1948 and began their ministry in Indonesia a year later. They remained there for the next thirty years.

Darlene died in 2004 at the age of eighty-six. Looking back on those first eight years of ministry in her book, *Evidence Not Seen*, Darlene said,

> Viewing those eight years from this far side, I marvel at the wisdom and love of our God, Who controls the curtains of the stage on which the drama of our lives is played; His hand draws aside the curtains of events only far enough for us to view one sequence at a time.

Had those eight years been revealed to me in one panoramic view that misty gray January morning in 1938, would I have had the courage to board the ship? I wonder. Through the intervening years, tempestuous winds of gale force have buffeted me. Waves of tidal proportions have threatened to carry me under or dash me upon the rocks. But knowing now what I did not know those many years ago, with C.H. Spurgeon, I can thank my God for every storm that has wrecked me upon the Rock, Christ Jesus![126]

Darlene's life is evidence the compensations for following the Lord far outweigh the cost. She felt her life, with the trials and hardships she faced, was to be envied by others. The Lord had been so patient with her and spent so much time with her through each trial she could confidently say, "Why anyone would be afraid to answer the call of being a missionary, I don't understand."[127] Darlene faced unthinkable, horrific hardships. In the end, she had more of her Lord, her greatest treasure. In the end, her life teaches us, the cost was worth it all.

ELISABETH ELLIOT

Life from Death
By Timera Kakish

If there is one name you may know when it comes to women in missions, it's Elisabeth Elliot. But do you know the details of her story? Hers is a story we can't afford to let fade in time. Because it's one thing to pack up your bag and move overseas to love people you've never met—it's another to return to a people who were responsible for your life's greatest tragedy.

Elisabeth Elliot's life is one filled with many bright days, but also very dark ones. Her determination to follow Jesus continues to influence generations of women around the world. Elisabeth's life is characterized by surrender, even when she faced tragedy and loss. Elisabeth willingly released control in order to give everything to God, to live a life that glorified Him.

"OBEDIENCE IS OUR TASK. THE RESULTS OF THAT OBEDIENCE ARE GOD'S, AND GOD'S ALONE."
- ELISABETH ELLIOT, URBANA, 1996

Elisabeth Elliot was born December 21, 1926, in Brussels, Belgium, to missionary parents. Before her first birthday she returned to the United States with her parents and siblings and settled near Philadelphia. As a child, Elisabeth noticed routines and patterns in her family that were different from many of her friends. Her parents taught Elisabeth what the Bible said and how they should follow it. They learned what God's Word said together as a family, and that practice instilled in Elisabeth a love for God's Word.[128]

Elisabeth learned early in her life God had a purpose for her, and His purpose was not just about her individual hopes and dreams. She learned God's purpose was much bigger than her plans; God was focused on the whole world.

Her family frequently hosted missionaries, which allowed her to learn about the global church and cross-cultural missions. Elisabeth grew to value missions. She became convinced she would one day serve as a missionary overseas.

When she was twelve, Elisabeth made a bold prayer of commitment and surrender to the Lord. She said,

> Lord, I give up all my own plans and purposes, all my own desires and hopes, and accept Thy will for my life. I give myself, my life, my all, utterly to Thee to be Thine forever. Fill me and seal me with thy Holy Spirit, use me as Thy wilt, send me where Thou wilt, work out Thy whole will in my life at any cost, now and forever.[129]

As Elisabeth transitioned to high school, she grew in her faith. She desired to have a Christian education. Elisabeth attended Hampden Dubose Academy, a private Christian school in Orlando, Florida. During this time, Elisabeth learned about Bible translation from a woman named Helen Yost. She was fascinated by the study of languages and excited at the possibility of translating the Bible for people who did not have it.

After graduating, she attended Wheaton College in Illinois. As Elisabeth settled into her studies at Wheaton, she started to think about marriage. She was confident God had placed a calling on her life to be a missionary; but she was unsure if there would be a man suitable for her to marry. Elisabeth asked God to help her see if there was anyone like-minded at Wheaton. Not long after, Elisabeth met Jim Elliot. He was also interested in missions. They built a friendship around their mutual passion for God's Word and His global mission.

During this time, she also made a transition from studying English to Greek in preparation to be a Bible translator. She wanted to pursue in-depth linguistics training after graduation, and an undergraduate degree in Greek seemed best. After graduation she spent time at the Summer Institute of Linguistics at the University of Oklahoma.

Elisabeth used her summer to study language techniques, specifically related to language translation among tribal groups. She wanted to help translate the Bible for people in tribal communities who were unreached.

Elisabeth experienced a lot of transition after college, but through it she maintained contact with Jim. They built a rich friendship. They cared for one another deeply, but loved the Lord and desired to honor Him above all else.[130]

LORD, I GIVE UP ALL MY OWN PLANS AND PURPOSES, ALL MY OWN DESIRES AND HOPES, AND ACCEPT THY WILL FOR MY LIFE. I GIVE MYSELF, MY LIFE, MY ALL, UTTERLY TO THEE TO BE THINE FOREVER.

In 1952, Elisabeth set out to be a single missionary in Ecuador. She settled in Quito, Ecuador, and focused all of her time on Bible translation. As Elisabeth settled into life in Quito, she realized how difficult Bible translation was, but she did not complain and did not regret her decision to move to Ecuador. She continued to submit to God, who she loved, and worked hard to translate the Bible for the native people in Quito.

Shortly after, Elisabeth transitioned to San Miguel, Ecuador, to work among a tribe called the Coloradoans. The Coloradoans did not have a written language, and Elisabeth wanted to work alongside the tribe to help them create one. Ultimately, this would allow them to translate the Bible to their native tongue.

At the time, Jim Elliot was also in Ecuador working in Shandia with a different people group. Almost a year after Elisabeth moved to Ecuador, Jim invited her to join him in Shandia to see the work he was doing.

After a long and sweet dating relationship, God confirmed Elisabeth and Jim would be effective ministers of the gospel as a married couple. In 1955, Jim and Elisabeth married in Quito, Ecuador. Their hearts' passion as individuals and as a couple was to share the gospel with those who had never heard. Jim and Elisabeth continued to serve through translating the Bible into native languages. They helped run a school for children, a church for the local believers, and a part-time medical clinic with other couples living in Shandia. In 1955, the Elliots had their first and only child, Valerie.

Later in 1955, Jim and several of his missionary friends began to reach out to a people group in a neighboring village: the Auca people. The Auca had never heard the gospel and had little to no contact with the surrounding tribes. Jim and four of his fellow missionaries, Ed McCully, Roger Youderian, Pete Fleming, and Nate Saint, planned to make contact with the Auca tribe in what they dubbed Operation Auca.[131] They knew the Auca were characterized by violence and were considered dangerous to outsiders. They were unsure of how the Auca would respond to them; however, they knew God led them to Ecuador to bring the good news of the gospel to the Auca.

Elisabeth and Jim's faith and confidence to trust God in this decision reveals much of their hearts. They knew not where this would lead, but they had determined to submit to God's will, not their own.

Jim and his companions spent the first several months of Operation Auca flying over the jungle to locate the tribe. Their pilot, Nate Saint, designed a way to lower a rope with a bucket from the plane to the Auca as they stood on an open beach. Nate would circle the plane overhead as they lowered the bucket. The Auca were able to get items in and out of the bucket. The goal was to make positive contact by giving small gifts to the Auca. Over the first few months, the Auca took the gifts and offered back other gifts. Soon, Jim and the others decided it was time to make physical contact. They set up camp down river from the beach they had flown over.

For the first time, these men made face-to-face contact with a few young Auca women and a young Auca man. Surprisingly, the young man motioned he wanted a ride in the plane! After the flight they told their families they planned to meet again with the Auca over the following days.

Elisabeth and the other families, would later find out the events that followed were primarily due to a miscommunication. Some of the tribal leaders were led to believe the missionary men intended to harm the women. The two women who had met them on the beach tried to convince the tribal leaders of their good intentions, but the tribal leaders were not deterred.

As the missionaries awaited contact with the Auca, something no one expected happened. On January 8, 1956, after making contact with the Auca people, Jim and his four companions were speared to death by men from the Auca tribe.[132]
Elisabeth and Jim had only been married for two and a half years when suddenly she was a widow! Their daughter Valerie was ten months old. Opposite of what one would assume of Elisabeth's heart amid her plight, she felt compassion for the people who killed him. She graciously stated, "the fact that Jesus Christ died for all makes me interested in salvation of all, but the fact that Jim loved and died for the Auca intensified my love for them."[133] After Jim's death, Elisabeth persevered. She personally committed herself to reaching the Auca people. She even even tried to move there. She knew the risk and counted the cost, and still pushed forward because obeying God was worth it. Elisabeth wrote in her journals,

> I prayed what seemed like a ridiculous prayer at the time of Jim's death, "Lord if there's anything you want me to do about the Auca, I'm available." God's leading was clear, there was something.[134]

Soon after the men's death, Elisabeth and Valerie, along with Nate Saint's sister Rachel, made contact with two Auca women in a Quichua village deep in the jungle. The two Auca women had come out from their remote village and settled in Quichua. Miraculously, the four women built a friendship. Shortly after

109

Elisabeth met the two Auca women, they invited her to come live in the village of Curaray to teach the Auca God's word. This was a significant event both for the Auca and Elisabeth. She knew that her safety would be at risk. She realized she was entering a violent community. Elisabeth did not let that deter her from submitting to God's larger plan: to bring salvation to the Auca people. As Elisabeth considered living among the Auca, she meditated on 2 Corinthians 4:11, "For we who live are always being given over to death for Jesus' sake so that the life of Jesus also may be revealed in our mortal body."[135]

In October 1958, Elisabeth, her now three-year-old daughter Valerie, and Rachel Saint moved to live with the Auca. They learned their language and formed a written language to aid in translating the Bible. Elisabeth and Rachel were resourceful, and with the help of a local Auca woman named Dayuma, they began the translation process. This was a most difficult task. It required a lot of patience and determination, but they would not give up.

After six years on the mission field, Elisabeth made the decision to take a short break. It was the first time she would returned to the United States since she left for Ecuador. It was also the first time she would go back since Jim's death. When she returned to the United States, she was stunned by the reception she received. The story of Jim's death and Elisabeth's reaction of love and forgiveness had inspired people all over the United States. Churches and pastors invited her to speak and share about her personal experience in Ecuador. Her story, which was filled with compassion and love for the lost, was a story of inspiration.

Just as Jesus died for the whole world and out of His death came life for all, so Elisabeth noted "life comes out of death" for the Auca tribe. Jim's death brought pain and sorrow, but it also brought salvation to the Auca people and inspired a generation in the United States. People saw God's mission was worth the cost of dying. Death in the service of God was worth it, because death was not the end. In Jesus, there is life everlasting.

After her time in the United States, Elisabeth returned to Ecuador for a few more years. What she saw encouraged her greatly. Many of the Auca people started to follow Jesus. She witnessed multiple baptisms of new believers from the Auca tribe, and her team completed the translation of a New Testament in the Auca language. A murderous tribe that just a short time ago had been hostile to all outsiders was now claiming Jesus as their King. Jim and his four friends' dream of bringing the gospel of hope to the Auca had been realized.[136]

Elisabeth dearly loved the people who had caused the death of her husband, and desired for them to know the true love of God. Her compassion for the Auca in the midst of pain and her obedience to God changed the lives of the Auca people for eternity. Elisabeth noted, "the will of God is always far different than we imagine, far bigger, far more difficult, but unspeakably more glorious."[137]

After eleven years on the field, Elisabeth returned to the United States permanently. She used her platform to inspire and challenge Christians in their faith to trust God and to follow Him with their whole lives. She published multiple books about the lessons God taught her in her time abroad, her relationship with Jim Elliot, and their work in Ecuador. She wanted people of all generations to read and be inspired by the things God did. She spoke at many conferences and churches and continued to impact the masses. Elisabeth Elliot died in 2015, at the age of eighty-eight.

Later in her life, Elisabeth noted to a group of women,

the women who make a difference will be those who have received the power of Christ and the scripture makes it very plain that the way in which we receive that power is through loss. Paul says, "I have suffered the loss of everything and count it garbage. All I care for is to know Christ." Emptiness, helplessness, loss, pain, transformable for the life of the world.[138]

THE WOMEN WHO MAKE A DIFFERENCE WILL BE THOSE WHO HAVE RECEIVED THE POWER OF CHRIST AND THE SCRIPTURE MAKES IT VERY PLAIN THAT THE WAY IN WHICH WE RECEIVE THAT POWER IS THROUGH LOSS.

Elisabeth Elliot knew, it's not in our own power and strength that we effect change in the world, but by surrendering to the power and love of Chris, even and *especially* in the face of our deepest loss.

Here I Am God, Send My Sister.

HELEN ROSEVEARE

A Privilege Mentality
By Rebecca Hickman

How many of us wonder if we could really pull off the whole "being a missionary" thing? When we sit down and really think of what it will cost us, the price can seem too high. This story shows us that is never the case.

As she stepped down from the platform at the Urbana '76 mission conference, Dr. Helen Roseveare's message lingered in the minds of the 17,000 university students in attendance.[139] She spoke from experience of the cost of declaring God's glory. Her long-term work as a medical missionary in Congo had prepared her for this moment. She shared of when, as a medical student at Cambridge, England, she herself attended a missions gathering and stood "along with several hundred others and declared publicly, 'I'll go anywhere God wants me to, whatever the cost.'"[140] She went on to say, in her endearing British accent,

...erwards, I went up into the mountains and had it out with God. "Ok, God, today I mean it. Go ahead; make me more like Jesus, whatever the cost. But please (knowing myself fairly well), when I feel I can't stand anymore and cry out, 'Stop!' would you ignore my 'stop' and remember that today I said 'Go!'? Well, He has graciously taken me at my word through the years."[141]

She challenged her audience to consider any cost they may face in following Christ as God's gracious hand, whittling away all that is not Christlike in them. She told of the personal costs God had asked of her while in the Congo, painfully but graciously stripping her of her subconscious racism and pride, as well as her "rights" to a husband, comfort, respect, health, and even her own safety.

For over forty years, Dr. Helen Roseveare traveled the world, speaking on the privilege of following Christ wherever He may lead. Her willingness to share her weaknesses and failures, the

authenticity in her story, and her boldness with truth from God's word drew in her listeners. Her descriptions of her candid interactions with God challenged others to consider their own relationship with Christ and what He was speaking specifically to them. At Urbana '76, she closed with this:

One word became unbelievably clear, and that word was "privilege." He didn't take away pain or cruelty or humiliation. No! It was all there, but now it was altogether different. It was with Him, for Him, in Him. He was actually offering me the inestimable privilege of sharing in some little way the edge of the fellowship of

His suffering... The cost suddenly seemed very small and transient in the greatness and permanence of the privilege.[142]

Many years later, Helen tells of her first night as a Christian, speaking in response to people with the genuine fear of suffering for Christ as a missionary:

> The evening I came to know the Lord Jesus as my Savior, I was overwhelmed at the wonder that God loved me, so much He sent Jesus to die for me. I was given a Bible, and Dr. Graham Scroggie wrote out Philippians 3:10 in the leaf... and he said to me, "Tonight, you have started this verse, 'that I may know Christ.' My prayer in the years that lie ahead is that you would know more and more of the power of His resurrection... And Helen, maybe one day God will give you the privilege of knowing something of the fellowship of His sufferings." I'd been a Christian for half an hour, and I was told that it was a privilege to suffer for Jesus!

HE WAS ACTUALLY OFFERING ME THE INESTIMABLE PRIVILEGE OF SHARING IN SOME LITTLE WAY THE EDGE OF THE FELLOWSHIP OF HIS SUFFERING... THE COST SUDDENLY SEEMED VERY SMALL.

Helen continued to recall her emotions as she realized how this moment impacted her,

> And that word "privilege" has stayed with me, I think possibly more than any one word in my Christian life ever since... It's a privilege that he saved me, it's a privilege that I have had any part in talking to others about Him. Everything has been privilege... I just fear that in today's climate, we – that's any of us to have

the privilege of speaking to others of Christ—we don't underline straight away that the Christian life will involve suffering... He himself said if we would follow Him, we must take up our cross; and He was going to Calvary! I believe the Savior suffers today, for the millions of unreached, untouched people who have never yet even heard his name. And He invites us – and it's such a privilege – to share with Him in His sufferings. I've got no way of saying you won't suffer. You will suffer. You should suffer, if you're really a Christian.[143]

I'D BEEN A CHRISTIAN FOR HALF AN HOUR, AND I WAS TOLD THAT IT WAS A PRIVILEGE TO SUFFER FOR JESUS!

When I reflect on her statements, I find within myself a longing to understand what she understood: the privilege of sharing in the fellowship of Christ's suffering. How can we begin to learn to have this "privilege mentality" in life, as Helen did? What produced this type of miraculous perspective within her? How had God shown her the immense privilege of suffering for His name? To understand these things, we must look back at the fuller story.

Helen Roseveare was born in 1925 in Hertfordshire, England, where her father taught at the local college. She grew up in an ordinary, middle-class family, but because education was a high priority for her father, Helen was sent to a prestigious all-girls school when she was twelve. She went on study medicine at Cambridge University. Going away to Cambridge, she decided to leave behind any ideas about believing in God. She'd had family members who had gone off to World War II and hadn't come back. She'd seen the brutality and cruelty of the war, and couldn't see how God could exist if He wasn't able to control what was happening in the world.

117

She did, however, continue to go to church every Sunday (just in case He was real) but nothing more. Helen admitted to feeling extremely lonely and frightened as a freshman. Without God in the picture, she realized it meant there were no limits in the world. She befriended a few Christian girls who were consistently kind and helpful to her. She saw they prayed to a God they knew. They invited her to join them for Bible studies and prayer meetings. She attended, but still she doubted. They shared the goodness of Christ with her during that first term. Over the winter break, Helen attended a Christian student event with them. What the speaker, Dr. Graham Scroggie, shared from Genesis and then Romans moved her. She felt desperate to know if God was real. Going back to her room alone, she prayed, "If there is a God, make Yourself known to me now."[144] She looked up and saw, "Be still and know that I am God..." (from Psalm 46:10) on the wall of her borrowed dorm room. She knew God had spoken to her personally in that place. From that moment, she understood God loved her dearly. She knew that very night she would go anywhere He asked and do anything He asked of her, being motivated by His love toward her.[145] She shared later on in life,

> The root motivation in me... [that] took me into Congo and kept me there... has always been the tremendous love of God for us individuals that we might so love others with His love that they too would come to know forgiveness of sins. This was reality—to allow God to put His love into us to love others. And I don't think I've ever bothered to think if it was easy or not. I just know I want to love others because He so loved me.[146]

AND I DON'T THINK I'VE EVER BOTHERED TO THINK IF IT WAS EASY OR NOT. I JUST KNOW I WANT TO LOVE OTHERS BECAUSE HE SO LOVED ME.

As a new Christian, her resolve became clear: to finish medical school and prepare herself for the mission field. It was far from easy. During this time, although they were allowed to take classes, women were not warmly welcomed in the medical profession. Her professors weren't pleasant toward her, and she didn't necessarily enjoy medicine. She knew this would help her serve others as a missionary, so she persevered. [147] After she graduated, Helen had still more schooling to complete. For six months, she studied at the Worldwide Evangelization Crusade (WEC) college. Once finished, she moved to Belgium to learn French. She then lived for a short time in Holland, taking a course on tropical diseases to be prepared for whatever lay ahead. This time spent in training seemed prolonged and tedious at times, but she knew it was essential for the work that God had prepared for her to do.

In March of 1953 at the age of 28, Helen was sent out from WEC Mission into the jungles of the Congo. She was finally a medical missionary after so many years of dreaming about it. She landed with high hopes, being extremely intelligent and efficient in her work. In that time period, single women missionaries were seen as second-class citizens on the mission field. However, as she jokingly explained, "Having more women than men doing the job out there, we used to have a saying in our mission: 'The woman is the man to do the job.'" [148]

In the Congo, the medical needs were overwhelming. She dreamed of establishing a training center where nurses would be taught the Bible and basic medicine and then sent back to their villages to handle routine cases, teach preventive medicine, and serve as lay evangelists. She didn't have approval from her fellow missionaries, who believed that medical training for nationals was not a valid use of time, but that evangelism and discipleship were more important. Moreover, her role as a woman physician quickly created struggles with her male colleagues and national coworkers. Despite the conflict, after only two years, she had built a combination hospital/training center in Ibambi, and her first four students had passed their government medical exams.

She was soon told she must relocate to Nebobongo, living in an old leprosy camp that had become overgrown by the jungle. Helen argued she must stay and continue the nursing training in Ibambi, but the mission's leadership insisted she move. Starting from scratch again, she built another hospital and continued training African nurses. During this time, she came to be known as "Mama Luka" to the Congolese, and she saw her womanhood as an advantage:

> As a woman in the Congo, I wasn't threatening to the local men, and being single, I had the time to serve. I truly enjoyed serving, as in serving others, I had a way of expressing my love for the Lord.[149]

Then, in 1957, the mission decided to relocate John Harris, a young British doctor, and his wife to Nebobongo and made him Helen's superior. Dr. Harris took charge of everything, even leading the Bible class that she'd taught. Helen felt pushed aside. She'd been her own boss for so long, and suddenly everything that had been hers was now his. This resulted in tension between them. Her strong-willed independence was her greatest strength, but also a definite weakness. She did not know how to submit to imperfect leadership. In 1958, after over a year of struggling with who was in control in Nebobongo, Helen left for a much needed home-leave in England. She was disillusioned with missionary work and felt like she might not return to the Congo.[150]

Back in England, she struggled with why she had such numerous issues between herself and the male leaders in the Congo. She began to convince herself the problem was her singleness. She made up her mind that what she needed was a doctor-husband to work with her and speak on her behalf. She asked God for a husband, telling Him she wouldn't go back as a missionary until she was married. During this time she met a young doctor and decided he would be the one. She bought new clothes, permed her hair, and resigned from WEC Mission, all to win his love. He did care for her, but not enough to marry her. Helen was heartbroken, mostly because she'd wasted so much time and money trying to force her plan into reality, without God.[151]

She began to embrace singleness, seeing it as another way to grow in Christlikeness. As she reflected on the life of Christ, she came to this conclusion:

Was Jesus satisfied? If Jesus was never married, with no wife or children, and was satisfied, then I can be satisfied single. God promises the best. It is a privilege; singleness is never a second-best. If He gives you the privilege of being single, it really is a wonderful privilege... And He has satisfied every need.[152]

Speaking of her singleness in hindsight (at the age of eighty-six), Helen recalled humorously,

IF JESUS WAS NEVER MARRIED, WITH NO WIFE OR CHILDREN, AND WAS SATISFIED, THEN I CAN BE SATISFIED SINGLE. IF HE GIVES YOU THE PRIVILEGE OF BEING SINGLE, IT REALLY IS A WONDERFUL PRIVILEGE.

Again, I was privileged. I fell in love with Jesus the night I was saved. It was the end of WWII and there were no fellows around. The only boys around were the drop-outs, the ones who were sick or wounded or frail, and we didn't want them anyway.[153]

As she traveled as a missions spokeswoman later in life, she would often speak at college campuses to Christian students. She said,

I would go into the girls' dorms to speak to them and they always wanted to know how I survived singleness. I've said naughtily to them: "Thank goodness for being single! Just praise the Lord! You see marrieds and their kids and some of the awful things they go through, and I've never had to go through all of that!"[154]

Still learning the privilege of singleness, Helen returned to the Congo in 1960. It was a tense time as the Congo sought independence from Belgium. Soon after Helen began her second term, independence was gained, which resulted in four years of civil war.[155] Many missionaries left because the risk was so high, but Helen had no plans of going back to England. She believed God had truly called her to the Congo, and He would protect her. She was again given charge of the medical base in Nebobongo and had countless opportunities to share Christ as she ministered in the midst of the turmoil. Through it all, she continued to learn how to see God in the details of her life and trust Him more fully. Still she dealt with bouts of depression, feeling she was failing as a Christian because she was so prone to spells of anger and bitterness along with other sins. God was continuing to whittle away all within her that was not Christlike.

As the rebels gained strength, reports came of missionaries being attacked. Helen endured a robbery and someone even tried to poison her, but always in her mind the situation was improving. Then, on August 15, 1964, the rebels took control of Nebobongo, and Helen was held in captivity along with her co-workers inside their hospital compound for the next five months. The food and medicine soon ran out. They clung to God for peace and strength to love their enemies, fighting their own battles against fear and hatred. She remembers,

> During the rebellion, I spoke to God, "I need you. I need you so desperately." I truly felt His arms around me that night. And during the imprisonment, I slept—nobody else did—I slept in the arms of Jesus. I felt safe in Him. His grace is sufficient. The verse He gave us during the rebellion was this: My grace is sufficient for you. My strength is made perfect in your weakness.[156]

On the night of October 29, rebel soldiers ransacked her house, found nothing, and then turned on her. They overpowered Helen in her small bungalow. She tried to escape, but they found her. Dragging her to her feet, they struck her over the head and shoulders, flinging her to the ground, striking her over and over again. Her back molars were kicked out by rebel boots. She was pushed back into her house by one soldier and then the unimaginable happened. Helen was brutally raped. She recalled that as she was forced down the hallway in her own home, she thought, "God, where are you? What is going on?"[157] She felt she was abandoned. However, in the next moment something happened. She suddenly realized God was indeed there. Not only there, but in full control. The enemy looked so very small compared to God. He said to her clearly, "Can you thank me? Can you thank Me for trusting you with this experience even if I never tell you why?" She was thinking, "No!" Then beyond comprehension in the midst of the darkness, she was able to say, "Yes, thank you."

> THE ENEMY LOOKED SO VERY SMALL COMPARED TO GOD. HE SAID TO HER CLEARLY, "CAN YOU THANK ME? CAN YOU THANK ME FOR TRUSTING YOU WITH THIS EXPERIENCE EVEN IF I NEVER TELL YOU WHY?"

Immediately, she was flooded with the enormous peace of God. She realized the rebels weren't fighting her, but Jesus in her! That truth revolutionized everything![158]

She knew God had given one word to her: "privilege." Philippians 3:10 came to her mind–"That I may know Christ and the power of His resurrection, and the privilege of the fellowship of His suffering."[159] She saw her suffering in comparison to the life she had in Christ. She was living out what Paul had written to the church in Corinth: "For this light momentary affliction is preparing for us an eternal weight of glory beyond all comparison" (2 Corinthians 4:17). Helen would suffer more physical and sexual brutality before her release. She found herself volunteering ahead of other women, so that she would take the torture before them. Her only desire was to somehow protect those who hadn't yet experienced the trauma of rape. God brought good out of these horrible experiences in her life as she counseled other single women missionaries who had been raped, as well. Helen knew her relationship with God had not been damaged. She actually felt more assured of His loving presence as a result of her suffering.

She later pointed to God's goodness, despite this great evil done against her. She said,

> Through the brutal heartbreaking experience of rape, God met with me—with outstretched arms of love. It was an unbelievable experience: He was so utterly there, so totally understanding, his comfort was so complete—and suddenly I knew—I really knew that his love was unutterably sufficient. He did love me! He did understand![160]

Throughout her life, she continued to help countless women who were trapped under the weight of false shame because of sexual abuse. Helen spoke toward this issue in an interview:

> We don't want to think about [rape]. We don't want to talk about it. We certainly don't talk about it in public or on the television screen... and yet, why? It's external. You're sinned against; it's not your sin. It can't touch your spirit, it's only your body... and suddenly [for women] to realize it's true... that [rape] can't get into my mind and my soul. I've helped girl after girl learn this truth; to be able to say yes to God as He asks them as well, "Can you thank Me for trusting you with this experience?"[161]

God sustained her through the numerous, violent beatings and sexual abuse, and on December 31, 1964, she and others were rescued. Helen had an initial sense of joy and relief, but also deep sorrow as she heard of her friends' martyrdom. During those years of war, at least 27 partnering missionaries were murdered, as well as over 200 nuns and priests. Besides all of these losses for Helen, over 250,000 of the African people, whom she lived for and loved, were killed. The healing process back in the UK began with three long months of depression and despair. It wasn't until Palm Sunday 1965, when she realized she wanted to go on living. God still had work for her to do in the Congo.[162]

In March of 1966, Helen made a decision that shocked everyone. After all she suffered, she decided to go back! Helen returned to Nebobongo for her third and final term. She soon moved to Nyankunde in northeastern Zaire to start a new medical center, working to establish a 250-bed hospital, complete with maternity ward, leprosy center, and a training college for doctors. She served as a missionary doctor for seven more years, but Congo had been changed by the war, and the people displayed a new sense of independence and nationalism. Because of this, her work was full of turmoil and disappointment as she faced conflict with students and co-workers. God used this struggle to again whittle away at the pride in her heart. Deep down, she wanted the respect and popularity that came with being a successful medical missionary. It never came. Even her farewell party was unexpectedly cancelled. Helen left Africa in 1973 due to health reasons, but she left with a broken spirit as well. In her mind, her twenty years of service in Africa seemed to have ended in defeat and discouragement, even though God had truly accomplished much through her.

When she returned to the UK, she went through an extremely lonely period in her life. Once again, she turned to God. He was all she had. Instead of bitterness in her heart, there came a new spirit of humility and a new appreciation for what Jesus had done for her on the cross. God was molding her for the next season of ministry. Helen became an internationally acclaimed spokeswoman for Christian missions. Her candid honesty was refreshing in a profession known for its super-sainthood. She mobilized Christians to the mission field by showing them God used imperfect people with real struggles to be His ambassadors to the unreached world. She was called upon to speak at Christian churches, conferences, and university groups all across the globe. She wrote numerous books, challenging her readers with the lessons God had faithfully and patiently taught her during her time in the Congo. As an elderly woman, she even led a mission trip to Cambodia and Vietnam.

Helen Roseveare went home to be with her Lord, for whom she counted it a privilege to suffer, on December 7, 2016, at the age of ninety-one. She is remembered for her love of Jesus, and "her passion for everyone else to know the Lord, asking complete strangers: 'My dear, did you know that Jesus loves you?'"[163] Helen's memorial service began with the reading of Philippians 3:7-14, her testimony clearly seen in Paul's writing: "Whatever gain I had, I count it as loss for the sake of Christ." Roger Carswell remembered,

> She was always self-deprecating, not speaking glowingly of herself, but looking to her Savior. She loved to speak about Jesus, and the way she used the name Jesus always brought a radiance to her face, a glow.[164]

From the beginning of her life in Christ to the very end, this verse, written in her first Bible as a new believer, was perhaps her most beloved guide: "I want to know Christ—yes, to know the power of His resurrection and participation in His sufferings, becoming like Him in His death..." (Philippians 3:10). This privilege mentality, defined by her life, is much more than just gritting one's teeth and enduring the trials of life. As followers of Christ, we are called to a vibrant relationship with Him. This involves actively and joyfully joining in His suffering, as we love the lost world around us. We

STIR ME, THAT I MAY STEP OUT OF THE APATHY AND INDIFFERENCE THAT SEEK TO OVERWHELM OUR SOCIETY.

have been commanded to proclaim the gospel, telling of God's love in sending Jesus to be our "suffering servant" (Isaiah 53), bringing salvation to ends of the earth (Isaiah 49:6). Are you willing to suffer alongside Christ so that the world can see His sacrificial love? Imagine what God would do through our generation if we—motivated by the great love of our Savior—were eager to go anywhere He asked, seeing it as a great privilege.

Helen's own prayer from July 1946 was prayed once more at her memorial service, as a prayer over the next generation of privileged believers:

> Stir me, dear God, to live for You in the very fullest sense, by the faith of Your dear Son, our Savior Jesus Christ. Stir me, that I may step out of the apathy and indifference that seek to overwhelm our society. Stir me to move out into the exciting... to see Jesus Christ at work in all the daily details of living. Give me the courage to believe and to act in faith, through Jesus Christ our Lord. Amen.[165]

Imagine what would happen if we prayed, as Helen did, to be stirred and moved into action. To actively join this God-given privilege of evangelizing the world in our generation, no matter the cost.

THEIR STORIES. YOUR STORY. HIS STORY.

What a legacy. What a tremendous group of women to have before us to encourage us, to exhort us, and to motivate us in our faith and dedication to the gospel!

These stories are our history. They tell us where we've been, but also where we are going as women who follow Jesus.

THESE STORIES ARE OUR HISTORY. THEY TELL US WHERE WE'VE BEEN, BUT ALSO WHERE WE ARE GOING AS WOMEN WHO FOLLOW JESUS.

So the question remains: Where are you going as a follower of Jesus? Are you following in the steps of these women of faith to go boldly to declare the gospel and our allegiance to King Jesus? Or will these stories simply fade in your memory as interesting pieces of the past? It is our prayer that these true stories will motivate and mobilize you; because the story doesn't end with this book, and it doesn't even end with you. It continues on. It's not just their story or our story, but God's story. And His story will last for eternity:

After this I looked, and behold, a great multitude that no one could number, from every nation, from all tribes and peoples and languages, standing before the throne and before the Lamb, clothed in white robes, with palm branches in their hands and crying out with a loud voice, "Salvation belongs to our God who sits on the throne, and to the Lamb!" (Revelation 7:9)

130

THREE RESOURCES TO HELP YOU TAKE YOUR NEXT STEP.

The Traveling Team

thetravelingteam.org

Find the greatest collection of mission resources, bible studies, articles and tools online at thetraveilngteam.org. Browse through thousands of timeless articles and updated information that will help you get started.

Mission Revolution

missionrev.org

Are you looking for speakers to help awaken your church or campus ministry? For over 15 years Mission Revolution has brought a new kind of mission conference to thousands all over the world, customized to your needs.

MissionAgency.org

missionagency.org

Are you feeling stuck and not knowing where to start? Let us match you with an opportunity in global mission. We help you work backward from God's mission to how you might fit with personal coaching and connecting from our staff who will help direct you to some of the best mission agencies in the world.

ENDNOTES

[1] James Knowles. *Memoir of Ann H. Judson, Late Missionary to Burmah.* Boston: Gould, Kendall and Lincoln, 1844, 15.

[2] Ibid., 12.

[3] Ibid., 13.

[4] Ruth Tucker. *From Jerusalem to Irian Jaya: A Biographical History of Christian Missions.* Grand Rapids, MI: Zondervan Publishing, 1983, 84.

[5] James D. Knowles, *Memoir of Ann H. Judson, Late Missionary to Burmah.* Boston: Gould, Kendall and Lincoln, 1844, 30-31.

[6] Ibid.

[7] Edward Judson. *The Life of Adoniram Judson.* Philadelphia: American Baptist Publication Society, 1883, 41.

[8] Ibid., 46.

[9] James D. Knowles, *Memoir of Ann H. Judson, Late Missionary to Burmah.* Boston: Gould, Kendall and Lincoln, 1844, 77-79.

[10] Ibid., 85-86.

[11] Ruth Tucker. *Guardians of the Great Commission: The Story of Women in Modern Missions.* Grand Rapids, MI: Zondervan, 1988, 24.

[12] Walter N Wyeth. *Ann H. Judson, A Memorial.* Cincinnati, OH: Aldine Printing, 1888, 96-97.

[13] Edward Judson, *The Life of Adoniram Judson.* Philadelphia, American Baptist Publication Society, 1883, 224.

[14] James D. Knowles, *Memoir of Ann H. Judson, Late Missionary to Burmah.* Boston: Gould, Kendall and Lincoln, 1844, 278.

[15] Eileen F. Moffett. "Betsey Stockton: Pioneer American Missionary." *International Bulletin of Missionary Research* 19.2 (April 1995):71.

[16] Ibid., 71.

[17] Ibid., 71.

[18] Ibid., 71.

[19] Ibid., 72.

[20] Alice T. Mott. "The 'Peculiar Case' of Betsey Stockton: Gender, Race, and the Role of an Assistant Missionary to the Sandwich Islands (1822-1825)." *Studies in World Christianity* 21.1 (March 2015):5.

[21] Ibid., 5.

[22] Eileen F. Moffett. "Betsey Stockton: Pioneer American Missionary." *International Bulletin of Missionary Research* 19.2 (April 1995):72.

[23] Ibid., 72.

[24] Alice T. Mott. "The 'Peculiar Case' of Betsey Stockton: Gender, Race, and the Role of an Assistant Missionary to the Sandwich Islands (1822-1825)." *Studies in World Christianity* 21.1 (March 2015):5.

[25] Ibid.

[26] Betsey Stockton. "Sandwich Island Mission." *The Christian Advocate* 1.2 (1823):88-89.

[27] Ibid.

[28] Ibid.

[29] Ibid.

[30] Betsey Stockton. "Sandwich Island Mission." *The Christian Advocate* 2.5 (1824): 232.

[31] Betsey Stockton. "Sandwich Island Mission." *The Religious Intelligencer* 9.14 (1821): 209-210.

[32] Ibid.

[33] Ibid.

[34] Alice T. Mott. "The 'Peculiar Case' of Betsey Stockton: Gender, Race, and the Role of an Assistant Missionary to the Sandwich Islands (1822-1825)." *Studies in World Christianity* 21.1 (March 2015):35.

[35] Eileen F. Moffett. "Betsey Stockton: Pioneer American Missionary." *International Bulletin of Missionary Research* 19.2 (April 1995):74.

[36] Janet and Geoff Benge. *Lottie Moon: Giving Her All for China.* Seattle,WA: YWAM Publishing, 2001, 41.

[37] Ibid., 49.

[38] Lottie Moon. "Lottie Moon: Letters and Quotes." *International Mission Board Resources.* IMB.org, "P'ingtu, China, January 9, 1889."

[39] Ibid.

[40] Ibid.

[41] Ibid.

[42] Janet and Geoff Benge. *Lottie Moon: Giving Her All for China.* Seattle,WA: YWAM Publishing, 2001, 148.

[43] Lottie Moon. "Lottie Moon: Letters and Quotes." *International Mission Board Resources.* IMB.org, "Tungchow, September 15, 1887."

[44] Elisabeth Elliot. *A Chance to Die, The Life and Legacy of Amy Carmichael.* Grand Rapids, MI: Revell Books, 1987, 19.

[45] Ibid., 26.

[46] Ibid., 31.

[47] Ibid., 35.

[48] Ibid., 37.

[49] Ibid., 41.

[50] Ibid., 54.

[51] Ibid., 55.

[52] Ibid., 55.

[53] Amy Carmichael. *Things As They Are: Missionary Work in Southern India.* New York: Fleming H. Revell, 1903, 158.

[54] Ruth Tucker. *From Jerusalem to Irian Jaya: A Biographical History of Christian Missions.* Grand Rapids, MI: Zondervan, 2004, 300.

[55] Elisabeth Elliot. *A Chance to Die, The Life and Legacy of Amy Carmichael.* Grand Rapids, MI: Revell Books, 1987, 287.

[56] Ibid., 79.

[57] Ruth Tucker. *From Jerusalem to Irian Jaya: A Biographical History of Christian Missions.* Grand Rapids, MI: Zondervan, 2004, 299.

[58] Elisabeth Elliot. *A Chance to Die, The Life and Legacy of Amy Carmichael.* Grand Rapids, MI: Revell Books, 1987, 100.

[59] Ibid., 126.

[60] Ibid., 121-22.

[61] Ibid., 165.

[62] Ibid., 183.

[63] Ibid., 185.

[64] Ibid., 258.

[65] Ibid., 190.

[66] Ibid., 274-75.

[67] Ibid., 377.

[68] "About Us: Dohnavur Family." *TheDohnavurFellowship.org,* (2013).

[69] Thomas A. Russell. *Women Leaders in the Student Christian Movement, 1880-1920.* Maryknoll, New York: Orbis Books, 2017.

[70] Bertha Conde. "The Missionary Call." *North American Students and World Advance: December 31, 1919, to January 4, 1920, Des Moines, Iowa,* edited by Burton St. John. New York: Student Volunteer Movement for Foreign Missions (1920): 286-87.

[71] John MacArthur. T*welve Extraordinary Women How God Shaped Women of the Bible and What He Wants to Do with You.* Nashville: Thomas Nelson, 2005, 17.

[72] "Deaths: Bertha Conde." *The Living Church* 109.10 (3 Sept. 1944):21.

[73] Thomas A. Russell. *Women Leaders in the Student Christian Movement, 1880-1920.* Maryknoll, New York: Orbis Books, 2017.

[74] Bertha Conde. "The Missionary Call." *North American Students and World Advance: December 31, 1919, to January 4, 1920, Des Moines, Iowa,* edited by Burton St. John. New York: Student Volunteer Movement for Foreign Missions, 1920, p 286-87.

[75] Ibid., 286-87.

[76] Ibid., 286-87.

[77] Ruth Franzen. *The Legacy of Ruth Rouse: International Bulletin of Missionary Research.* Stockholm: Triangelforlaget, 1939.

[78] Ibid.

[79] Ibid.

[80] Ibid.

[81] Ibid.

[82] Thomas A. Russell. *Women Leaders in the Student Christian Movement, 1880-1920.* Maryknoll, New York: Orbis Books, 2017.

[83] Ruth Rouse. "The Students and the Modern Missionary Crusade." *Fifth International Convention of the Student Volunteer Movement for Foreign Missions, 28 February - 4 March, 1906, Nashville Tennessee.* Student Volunteer Movement for Foreign Missions, 262-263.

[84] Ruth Rouse. "Make Jesus King." *The Report of the International Students Missionary Conference, 1 January - 5 January, 1896. Liverpool.* London: The Student Volunteer Missionary Union, 1896.

[85] Ruth Franzen. *The Legacy of Ruth Rouse: International Bulletin of Missionary Research.* Stockholm: Triangelforlaget, 1939.

[86] Thomas A. Russell. *Women Leaders in the Student Christian Movement, 1880-1920.* Maryknoll, New York: Orbis Books, 2017.

[87] Ruth Rouse. "The Students and the Modern Missionary Crusade." *Fifth International Convention of the Student Volunteer Movement for Foreign Missions, 28 February - 4 March, 1906, Nashville Tennessee.* Student Volunteer Movement for Foreign Missions, 268.

[88] Thomas A. Russell. *Women Leaders in the Student Christian Movement, 1880-1920.* Maryknoll, New York: Orbis Books, 2017.

[89] Ruth Franzen. *The Legacy of Ruth Rouse: International Bulletin of Missionary Research.* Stockholm: Triangelforlaget, 1939.

[90] Thomas A. Russell. *Women Leaders in the Student Christian Movement, 1880-1920.* Maryknoll, New York: Orbis Books, 2017.

[91] Ruth Rouse "An Appeal to Women Students for Missionary Decision." *The Intercollegian, Fourth Series* 23:7 (April 1901):151.

[92] "Grace Wilder." *Biographical Dictionary of Christian Missions.* edited by Gerald H. Anderson. Grand Rapids, Michigan: William B. Eerdmans Publishing, 1999.

[93] Jessica Ahrend. "History of Mission: Grace Wilder." *The Traveling Team.* *www.*TheTravelingTeam.org.

[94] Ibid.

[95] Johanna M. Selles. "The Role of Women in the Formation of the World Student Christian Federation." *International Bulletin of Missionary Research* 30.4 (Oct. 2006):189-194.

[96] Ibid.

[97] Jessica Ahrend. "History of Mission: Grace Wilder." *The Traveling Team.* *www.*TheTravelingTeam.org.

[98] Tissington Tatlow. *The Story of the Student Christian Movement of Great Britain and Ireland.* London: Student Christian Movement Press, 1933.

[99] Jessica Ahrend. "History of Mission: Grace Wilder." *The Traveling Team.* *www.*TheTravelingTeam.org.

[100] "Grace Wilder." *Biographical Dictionary of Christian Missions.* edited by Gerald H. Anderson. Grand Rapids, Michigan: William B. Eerdmans Publishing, 1999.

[101] Grace Wilder. "Shall I Go?" *Thoughts for Girls* 5th Ed. New York: Student Volunteer Movement for Foreign Missions, 1888.

[102] Ibid.

[103] Ibid.

[104] Grace Wilder. "The Student Missionary Appeal: Village Settlements." *The Student Missionary Appeal: Addresses at the Third International Convention of the Student Volunteer Movement for Foreign Missions, Cleveland, Ohio, 1898.* New York: Student Volunteer Movement for Foreign Missions, 1898.

[105] Jessica Ahrend. "History of Mission: Grace Wilder." *The Traveling Team.* www.TheTravelingTeam.org.

[106] Leslie Ludy. "Esther Ahn Kim: The Power of Suffering Well for Christ." *Set Apart Girl* (1 March 2014) SetApartGirl.com.

[107] Esther Ahn Kim. *If I Perish.* Chicago: Moody Bible Institute, 1977, 27.

[108] Ibid., 71.

[109] Ibid., 47.

[110] Ibid., 58.

[111] Ibid., 60.

[112] Ibid., 50.

[113] Ibid., 70.

[114] Ibid., 139.

[115] Ibid., 249.

[116] Ibid., 257.

[117] Ibid., 257.

[118] Darlene Diebler Rose. *Evidence Not Seen: A Woman's Miraculous Faith in the Jungles of World War II.* New York, NY: HarperCollins, 1988, 47.

[119] Ibid., 35.

[120] Ibid., 41.

[121] Ibid., 45.

[122] Ibid., 70.

[123] Ibid., 70.

[124] Ibid., 70.

[125] Ibid., 155-56.

[126] Ibid., 221-22.

[127] David Flang. "Darlene Rose – POW WWII." *YouTube* (18 Jan. 2007).

[128] Janet and Geoff Benge. *Elisabeth Elliot: Joyful Surrender.* Seattle, WA: YWAM Publishing, 2010.

[129] Elisabeth Elliot. "Women That Make a Difference." *Sermon Library, YouTube* (22 Nov. 2017).

[130] Elisabeth Elliot. *Passion and Purity.* Grand Rapids, MI: Fleming H. Revell, 1984.

[131] Elisabeth Elliot. *Through Gates of Splendor.* Lincoln, NE: Back to Bible Broadcasts, 1957.

[132] Ibid.

[133] Janet and Geoff Benge. *Elisabeth Elliot: Joyful Surrender.* Seattle, WA: YWAM Publishing, 2010.

[134] Elisabeth Elliot. "Elisabeth Elliot Testimony Urbana 1996." *Urbana Missions, YouTube* (16 June 2015).

[135] Ibid.

[136] Janet and Geoff Benge. *Elisabeth Elliot: Joyful Surrender.* Seattle, WA: YWAM Publishing, 2010.

[137] Elisabeth Elliot. "Elisabeth Elliot Testimony Urbana 1996." *Urbana Missions, YouTube* (16 June 2015).

[138] Elisabeth Elliot. "Women That Make a Difference." *Sermon Library, YouTube* (22 Nov. 2017).

[139] Urbana is a major Christian student missions conference that began in 1946. Urbana is held once every three years, hosted by InterVarsity Christian Fellowship. Urbana.org.

[140] Helen Roseveare. "Urbana '76: Declare His Glory Among the Nations." *InterVarsity Christian Fellowship (*1976). Urbana.org/urbana-76.

[141] Ibid.

[142] Ibid.

[143] "Question Panel with John Piper, Randy Alcorn, and Helen Roseveare." *SermonIndex, YouTube* (19 June 2012).

[144] Moira Brown. "Why Does a God of Love Allow Suffering." *100huntley, YouTube* (11 May 2011).

[145] Helen Roseveare. "That We Might So Love Others." *WEC International.* www.WEC-USA.org.

[146] Ibid.

[147] David Meredith. "An Interview with Dr. Helen Roseveare." *Christian Focus, YouTube* (6 November 2011).

[148] Ibid.

[149] Helen Roseveare. "Have You Fallen in Love with Jesus." *100ofthose, YouTube* (1 June 2010).

[150] Nöel Piper. *Faithful Women and Their Extraordinary God.* Wheaton, Illinois: Crossway Books, 2005.

[151] Ibid.

[152] Ron Brown. "Dr. Helen Roseveare on Singleness." *CRDAfrica, YouTube* (20 August 2011).

[153] Justin Taylor. "A Woman of Whom the World Was Not Worthy: Helen Roseveare (1925-2016)." *The Gospel Coalition* (7 December 2016) www.TheGospelColaition.org.

[154] Ron Brown. "Dr. Helen Roseveare on Singleness." *CRDAfrica, YouTube* (20 August 2011).

[155] Moira Brown. "Why Does a God of Love Allow Suffering." *100huntley, YouTube* (11 May 2011).

[156] Ron Brown. "Dr. Helen Roseveare on Singleness." *CRDAfrica, YouTube* (20 August 2011).

[157] Moira Brown. "Why Does a God of Love Allow Suffering." *100huntley, YouTube* (11 May 2011).

[158] Ibid.

[159] Ibid.

[160] Justin Taylor. "A Woman of Whom the World Was Not Worthy: Helen Roseveare (1925-2016)." *The Gospel Coalition* (7 December 2016) www.TheGospelCoalition.org.

[161] Moira Brown. "Why Does a God of Love Allow Suffering." *100huntley, YouTube* (11 May 2011).

[162] Ibid.

[163] "Funeral of Helen Roseveare." *Peter Mackey, YouTube* (13 December 2016).

[164] Ibid.

[165] Ibid.

BIBLIOGRAPHY

Ann Judson

Judson, Edward. *The Life of Adoniram Judson.* Philadelphia: American Baptist
        Publication Society, 1883.

Knowles, James. *Memoir of Ann H. Judson, Late Missionary to Burmah.* Boston: Gould,
        Kendall and Lincoln, 1844.

Tucker, Ruth. *From Jerusalem to Irian Jaya: A Biographical History of Christian Missions.*
        Grand Rapids, MI: Zondervan Publishing, 1983.

Tucker, Ruth. *Guardians of the Great Commission: The Story of Women in Modern
        Missions.* Grand Rapids, MI: Zondervan, 1988.

Wyeth, Walter N. *Ann H. Judson, A Memorial.* Cincinnati, OH: Aldine Printing, 1888.

Betsey Stockton

"Betsey Stockton." *Biographical Dictionary of Christian Missions.* edited by Gerald H.
        Anderson. Grand Rapids, Michigan: William B. Eerdmans Publishing, 1999.

Johnson, Sarah and Eileen Moffett. "Lord, Send Us: A Kaleidoscope of Evangelists."
        Christian History and Biography 90, (2006):35-38.

Moffett, Eileen F. "Betsey Stockton: Pioneer American Missionary." *International
        Bulletin of Missionary Research* 19.2 (April 1995):71.

Ott, Alice T. "The 'Peculiar Case' of Betsey Stockton: Gender, Race, and the Role of an
        Assistant Missionary to the Sandwich Islands (1822-1825)." *Studies in World
        Christianity* 21.1 (March 2015):4-19.

Stockton, Betsey. "Sandwich Island Mission." *The Christian Advocate* 1.2 (1823):88-89.
        *American Antiquarian Society (AAS) Historical Periodicals Collection: Series
        2,* EBSCOhost (accessed February 22, 2018).

Stockton, Betsey. "Sandwich Island Mission." *The Christian Advocate* 2.5 (1824): 232.
        *American Antiquarian Society (AAS) Historical Periodicals Collection: Series
        2,* EBSCOhost (accessed February 7, 2018).

Stockton, Betsey. "Sandwich Island Mission." *The Religious Intelligencer* 9.14 (1821): 209-210. *American Antiquarian Society (AAS) Historical Periodicals Collection: Series 2*, EBSCOhost (accessed February 7, 2018).

Lottie Moon

Benge, Janet and Geoff. *Lottie Moon: Giving Her All for China.* Seattle,WA: YWAM Publishing, 2001.

Moon, Lottie. "Lottie Moon: Letters and Quotes." *International Mission Board Resources.* https://store.imb.org/lottie-moon-letters-quotes-download.

Amy Carmichael

"About Us: Dohnavur Family." *TheDohnavurFellowship.org,* (2013).

Carmichael, Amy. *Things As They Are: Missionary Work in Southern India.* New York: Fleming H. Revell, 1903, 158.

Elliot, Elisabeth. *A Chance to Die, The Life and Legacy of Amy Carmichael.* Grand Rapids, MI: Revell Books, 1987

Tucker, Ruth. *From Jerusalem to Irian Jaya: A Biographical History of Christian Missions.* Grand Rapids, MI: Zondervan, 2004.

Bertha Conde

Conde, Bertha. "The Missionary Call." *North American Students and World Advance: December 31, 1919, to January 4, 1920, Des Moines, Iowa,* edited by Burton St. John. New York: Student Volunteer Movement for Foreign Missions, 1920.

"Deaths: Bertha Conde." *The Living Church* 109.10 (3 Sept. 1944):21.

MacArthur, John. *Twelve Extraordinary Women How God Shaped Women of the Bible and What He Wants to Do with You.* Nashville: Thomas Nelson, 2005, 14-17.

Russell, Thomas A. *Women Leaders in the Student Christian Movement, 1880-1920.* Maryknoll, New York: Orbis Books, 2017.

Ruth Rouse

Franzen, Ruth. *The Legacy of Ruth Rouse: International Bulletin of Missionary Research.* Stockholm: Triangelforlaget, 1939.

Rouse, Ruth, "An Appeal to Women Students for Missionary Decision." *The Intercollegian, Fourth Series* 23:7 (April 1901):151.

Rouse, Ruth. "Make Jesus King." *The Report of the International Students Missionary Conference, 1 January - 5 January, 1896.* Liverpool. London: The Student Volunteer Missionary Union, 1896.

Rouse, Ruth. "The Students and the Modern Missionary Crusade." *Fifth International Convention of the Student Volunteer Movement for Foreign Missions, 28 February - 4 March, 1906.* Nashville Tennessee. Student Volunteer Movement for Foreign Missions.

Russell, Thomas A. *Women Leaders in the Student Christian Movement, 1880-1920.* Maryknoll, New York: Orbis Books, 2017.

Grace Wilder

Ahrend, Jessica. "History of Mission: Grace Wilder." *The Traveling Team.* http://www.thetravelingteam.org/articles/grace-wilder

Braisted, Ruth Evelyn Wilder. *In This Generation: The Story of Robert P. Wilder.* New York: Friendship Press, 1941.

Goldsmith, Elizabeth. *Roots and Wings: Five Generations and Their Influence.* Waynesboro, GA: Paternoster Publishing Publication, 1998.

"Grace Wilder." *Biographical Dictionary of Christian Missions.* edited by Gerald H. Anderson. Grand Rapids, Michigan: William B. Eerdmans Publishing, 1999.

Selles, Johanna M. "The Role of Women in the Formation of the World Student Christian Federation." *International Bulletin of Missionary Research* 30.4 (Oct. 2006):189-194.

Tatlow, Tissington. *The Story of the Student Christian Movement of Great Britain and Ireland.* London: Student Christian Movement Press, 1933.

Wallstrom, Timothy C. *The Creation of a Student Movement to Evangelize the World.* Pasadena, CA: William Carey International University Press, 1980.

Wilder, Grace. "Shall I Go?" *Thoughts for Girls* 5th Ed. New York: Student Volunteer Movement for Foreign Missions, 1888.

Wilder, Grace. "The Student Missionary Appeal: Village Settlements." *The Student Missionary Appeal: Addresses at the Third International Convention of the Student Volunteer Movement for Foreign Missions, Cleveland, Ohio, 1898.* New York: Student Volunteer Movement for Foreign Missions, 1898.

Esther Ahn Kim

Kim, Esther Ahn. *If I Perish.* Chicago: Moody Bible Institute, 1977.

Ludy, Leslie. "Esther Ahn Kim: The Power of Suffering Well for Christ." *Set Apart Girl* (1 March 2014) https://setapartgirl.com/magazine/article/03-1-14/esther-ahn-kim.

Darlene Diebler Rose

Akin, Daniel. "Darlene Diebler Rose: Unwavering Faith in God's Promises." *International Mission Board* (10 May 2017). https://www.imb.org/2017/05/10/darlenedieblerrose.

"Darlene Rose Obituary: Missionary Author was Captured by Japanese in World War II." *The Chattanoogan* (29 Feb. 2004). http://www.chattanoogan.com/2004/2/29/47410/Rose-Darlene.aspx.

Flang, David. "Darlene Rose – POW WWII." *YouTube* (18 Jan. 2007).

Henry, W. K.. "Darlene Diebler Rose." *Darlene Diebler Rose: A Woman of Faith* (Jan. 2007) http://darlenerose.org/index.html.

"Incredible Testimony of Missionary Darlene Rose." *Mountain Lodge Pentecostal Church, YouTube* (22 September 2016).

Rose, Darlene Diebler. *Evidence Not Seen: A Woman's Miraculous Faith in the Jungles of World War II.* New York, NY: HarperCollins, 1988.

"Russell Diebler: Indonesia 1930-1934." *The Alliance.* https://www.cmalliance.org/about/history/in-the-line-of-fire/diebler.

Elisabeth Elliot

Benge, Janet and Geoff. *Elisabeth Elliot: Joyful Surrender.* Seattle, WA: YWAM Publishing, 2010.

Elliot, Elisabeth. "Elisabeth Elliot Testimony Urbana 1996." *Urbana Missions, YouTube* (16 June 2015).

Elliot, Elisabeth. *Passion and Purity.* Grand Rapids, MI: Fleming H. Revell, 1984.

Elliot, Elisabeth. *Through Gates of Splendor.* Lincoln, NE: Back to Bible Broadcasts, 1957.

Elliot, Elisabeth. "Women That Make a Difference." *Sermon Library, YouTube* (22 Nov. 2017).

Helen Roseveare

Brown, Moira. "Why Does a God of Love Allow Suffering." *100huntley, YouTube* (11 May 2011).

Brown, Ron. "Dr. Helen Roseveare on Singleness." *CRDAfrica, YouTube* (20 August 2011).

"Funeral of Helen Roseveare." *Peter Mackey, YouTube* (13 December 2016).

Meredith, David. "An Interview with Dr. Helen Roseveare." *Christian Focus, YouTube* (6 November 2011).

Piper, Nöel. *Faithful Women and their Extraordinary God.* Wheaton, Illinois: Crossway Books, 2005.

"Question Panel with John Piper, Randy Alcorn, and Helen Roseveare." *SermonIndex.net, YouTube* (19 June 2012).

Roseveare, Helen. *Give Me this Mountain.* United Kingdom: Christian Focus Publishing, 1966.

Roseveare, Helen. "Have You Fallen in Love with Jesus." *10ofthose, YouTube* (1 June 2010).

Roseveare, Helen. "That We Might So Love Others." *WEC International.* https://www.wec-usa.org/send-2.

Roseveare, Helen. "Urbana '76: Declare His Glory Among the Nations." *InterVarsity Christian Fellowship (*1976). https://urbana.org/urbana-76.

Taylor, Justin. "A Woman of Whom the World Was Not Worthy: Helen Roseveare (1925-2016)." *The Gospel Coalition* (7 December 2016). https://thegospelcoalition.org/blogs.

Tucker, Ruth. *From Jerusalem to Irian Jaya: A Biographical History of Christian Missions.* Grand Rapids, MI: Zondervan Publishing, 1983.